# The Story of FURNITURE

Highboy in the Chippendale style made in Philadelphia and showing a pleasing combination of detailed carving and rich mahogany. About 1770.

The
Story of
FURNITURE

Julia Raynsford

**Hamlyn**

London · New York · Sydney · Toronto

# Preface

Published by
The Hamlyn Publishing Group Limited
London · New York · Sydney · Toronto
Astronaut House, Feltham, Middlesex
England
© Copyright The Hamlyn Publishing
Group Limited 1975

ISBN 0 600 38174 9

Phototypeset in England by
Keyspools Limited, Golborne, Lancashire
Printed in Hong Kong by
Leefung-Asco Printers Limited

This book is an attempt to present a basic but well illustrated introduction to the history of Western furniture and is intended for those people who are drawn to the subject but have little or no previous knowledge. In a book of this size such a wide subject cannot be treated in depth, and those seeking a more profound understanding of the development of furniture should consult *World Furniture*, edited by Mrs Helena Hayward, which covers the whole subject with great scholarship and in very much more detail. For those who find their interest aroused by the furniture made in a particular century, style or country, a host of specialised books exist to which they may turn.

*Julia Raynsford*

## Acknowledgments

I wish to express my thanks to my colleagues in the Department of Furniture and Woodwork of the Victoria and Albert Museum for all their help and encouragement, especially to Mr Peter Thornton, Keeper of the Department, and to Mr John Hardy and Mr Clive Wainwright who have been more than generous with their time and knowledge. My thanks are also due to Mrs Helena Hayward who for many years has given me so much help and guidance. Finally I should like to thank my father for reading the text and contributing so many valuable suggestions.

### Illustrations
The illustration on page 47 is reproduced by gracious permission of Her Majesty the Queen.

### Sources of black and white illustrations
A.G.L., Brussels. 69; Alinari, 13, 14 left, 21; Bayer. Vervaltung der Staatlichen Schlösser und Gärten, Munich 65 right; Bibliothèque Nationale, Paris, 24 bottom; Bodleian Library, Oxford, 97 bottom; Colonel and Mrs Miodrag R. Blagojevich, 76; Marcel Breuer and Associates, New York, 119 right; Brogi, 19 right; Caisse Nationale des Monuments Historiques, Paris 84; Christie, Manson and Woods, 97 top; Civici Musei Veneziani d'Arte e di Storia, 36 left; *Connaissance des Arts*, 41; *Country Life*, 49; R. Fortt, Kingston, 99 right; John R. Freeman & Co. Ltd, 17 top right, 32 left, 33, 72; Freneria, Barcelona, 16; Frick Collection, New York, 23 bottom; Gabinetto Fotografio Nazionale, Rome, 34 left; Glasgow Art Gallery and Museum, 45 right; Hamlyn Group Picture Library, 15 top, 20 top, 25 left, 29 right, 39 right, 48, 60 left, 61 top, 62, 96, 109 top, 109 bottom, 110, 117 top, 117 bottom, 121 top, 121 bottom; Henry Francis du Pont Winterthur Museum, Winterthur, Delaware, 80–81; L. H. Hildyard, 32 right; Jacqueline Hyde, Paris, 42–43, 56 bottom, 57 bottom, 85 top; A. F. Kersting, London, 17 bottom right, 45 top; Landsmuseum für Kunst, Münster, 26 bottom, 28–29; Louvre, Paris, 93; Lyndhurst. The National Trust for Historic Preservation in the United States, 116 bottom; Metropolitan Museum of Art, New York, 72, 73, 77, 105; Musée des Arts Décoratifs, Paris, 42 left, 57 top, 88 top, 113 top, 113 centre, 113 bottom; Museo de Artes Decorativos, Madrid, 24 top; Musée Carnavalet, Paris, 15 bottom; Musée Camondo de Nissim, Paris, 58 left, 85 bottom, 89; Museo Nacional de Arte Antiga, Lisbon, 52; Museum of the City of New York, 101, 104, 116 top; National Trust, 53; Photographie Giraudon, Paris, 40; Rijksmuseum, Amsterdam, 30 left, 30 bottom right, 36 right, 37, 56 top, 59 bottom, 88 bottom; Royal Pavilion, Brighton, 100 top; Russell de Sowza, Oporto, 68; C. E. Sparcie, 92; Roger Stertevant, 120–121; Teigens, Oslo, 25 right; Temple Newsam House, Leeds, 50–51; Bertram Unné, Harrogate, 100 bottom; Upsala University, Sweden, 28 left; Vervaltung der Staatlichen Schlössen und Gärten, Berlin, 101; Victoria and Albert Museum, London, 17 left, 20 bottom, 31 bottom, 44–45, 60–61, 108 bottom, 112 top, 112 bottom; Verlag Gunderman, Würzburg, 64–65, 66 bottom; Roger Wood, London, 12.

### Sources of colour illustrations
American Museum, Bath, 114–115; L. Aufsberg, Sonthofen in Allgaü, 26 top; Bibliothèque Nationale, Paris, 91; Christie, Manson and Woods, 83; Cooper Bridgeman Library, 58–59, 62, 115 right; Hamlyn Group Picture Library, 10, 27, 30–31, 43, 50, 54–55, 62, 66, 94 top, 94 bottom, 95, 106–107, 110, 111, 122–123; Henry Francis du Pont Winterthur Museum, Winterthur, Delaware, 70–71, 74 bottom, 78 left, 78–79, 98, 103; Jacqueline Hyde, Paris, 42–43, 86; Index of American Design, 74 top, 75; F. L. Kennett, London, 11; A. F. Kersting, London, 90; Museum für Kunsthandwerk, Frankfurt am Main, 46; Philadelphia Museum of Art, 22; Photographie Giraudon, Paris, 14–15, 87; *Réalités*, 63, 82; Reunion des Musées Nationaux, Paris, 47; Rijksmuseum, Amsterdam, 38–39, 114; Scala, Antella, 18–19, 23 top, 34–35, 51, 67; Sotheby Parke Bernet, New York, 5; Stedelijk Museum, Amsterdam, 118–119; White House Historical Association, 102.

# Contents

## Egypt

Our knowledge of Egyptian furniture is derived not only from numerous examples to be seen in paintings, sculptures and tomb reliefs but also from a number of actual pieces which have been preserved in relatively good condition thanks to the Egyptian custom of burying with the dead their personal and household possessions and to the exceptionally dry climate of Upper Egypt.

Materials and ornamental techniques were varied and imaginative. The art of veneering had been known at least as early as 3000 BC, and while acacia, sycamore and tamarisk were among the indigenous woods generally used, imported woods such as ebony, cedar and juniper are also commonly found on high quality furniture. Ivory and silver were often introduced into marquetry and inlay decoration, and gold leaf applied to gesso was increasingly used from the time of the New Kingdom (about 1575–1075 BC). Tools were rudimentary, but the Egyptian joiner knew how to make dovetail and mortice-and-tenon joints, while the corners of such pieces as stools and bed frames were mitred or simply bound with cords.

The stool had been developed into a valued article of furniture by the time of the Middle Kingdom (2050–1785 BC), and surviving examples show a high level of craftsmanship and a wide variety of design, indicating that at this time the stool was the accepted seat of the rich. The chair became more familiar from about 1600 BC, the earlier examples having straight backs and arms reaching to armpit level. Later chairs have less awkward proportions, and those with sloping rounded backs were certainly designed for greater comfort. The seat was generally made of woven cords, or

This detail, from an Attic red-figure vase found at Vulci in Etruria, illustrates a klismos chair. About 440 BC.

animal skins stretched over the framework.

The bed was regarded as an important piece of furniture, and among those that have survived are some fine examples found in the tomb of Tutankhamun. One of these has two sides formed of long slim cows, while another folds in the manner of a camp bed. A bed dating from the Old Kingdom (2700–2200 BC) illustrates the characteristic way in which the framework was made higher at the head than at the foot and was sup-

ported on short animal legs. Many Egyptian beds had elaborately decorated footboards, but the only support for the head appears to have been a crescent-shaped device.

The Egyptians did not make large tables, their needs being met by small stands of papyrus, wood, pottery or metal. Special stands were made to support games boards, such as the example from the tomb of Tutankhamun which features feline paws raised on golden drums resting on an ebony

Box-on-stand in which fine linen was stored. From the Tomb of Tutankhamun (18th Dynasty). Cairo Museum.

sledge. Games boards, as in this case, often have a drawer for containing the playing pieces, but curiously enough neither chests-of-drawers nor cupboards were developed by the Egyptians. Boxes and cabinets, however, varied greatly in shape and size and were designed to contain all manner of objects from wigs and trinkets to linen and clothing.

# Greece

Virtually no furniture has survived from Ancient Greece, but its development can be traced through the study of vase paintings and relief sculpture. Many forms were inherited from Egypt but adapted to suit the Greeks' way of life. At meal-times, for instance, they reclined elegantly on couches, but these had now lost the footboard and headrest, although like the Egyptian examples they were often beautifully decorated with metal, inlay and ivory. The food was served from small portable tables frequently round in form and supported on a tripod or on three slender animal legs.

On seat furniture, animal legs gradually became less common and were replaced by rectangular or turned supports. Sometimes they were decorated with painted or inlaid palmettes. Seats in the throne-like tradition were often vigorously carved with animal and bird forms and with motifs typical of the classical repertoire of ornament, such as the rosette, anthemion and key pattern. In contrast to these substantial and sculptural seats, a chair of great charm and elegance with curving legs and backboard was to become, by the 5th century BC, one of the most popular pieces of household furniture. It is described as the klismos and, like the X-frame folding stool and the tripod table, was to provide a model for furniture designers some 1800 years later.

# Rome

The Egyptians and Greeks used chests in which to store their belongings, and it was the Romans who were the first to develop cupboards with shelves and panelled doors. The Romans also designed more substantial tables of which some marble and stone examples were of splendidly sculptural form. New types of seat also emerged, such as the round-backed wickerwork chair and the panelled bench.

The Romans were also responsible for introducing certain modifications to the Greek prototypes on which their furniture was primarily based. The klismos, for instance, evolved a heavier form, and from the end of the first century AD the Roman couch so often depicted on tomb sculpture had a higher back and sides. As in Greece, footstools were frequently made to accompany the seat furniture.

The Barbarian invasions of Roman Italy obscured but did not entirely extinguish Classical art forms and ornament, which happily survived, however tenuously, to provide inspiration for countless artists and designers in later centuries.

Bed and armchair from the Tomb of Queen Hetepheres. Old Kingdom (4th Dynasty). Cairo Museum.

Marble table support. 1st century AD.
House of Cornelius Rufus, Pompeii.

# The Middle Ages
## about AD 500 - about 1400

As of previous periods, our knowledge of early medieval and Romanesque furniture has had to be culled from contemporary illustrations, inventories and wills because practically no pieces which can be confidently dated earlier than AD 1200 have survived.

After the fall of Rome some Classical furniture styles were preserved in Byzantium (Constantinople) where the standards of craftsmanship were not disrupted by the Barbarian invasions. Here the lighter curving forms of Rome gave way to a more formal architectural tradition exemplified by the magnificent 6th-century Byzantine chair known as the 'Throne of Maximian'. Made of ivory, it is carved in high relief to represent the Apostles, St John the Baptist and scenes from the life of Christ.

'Throne of Maximian'. Byzantine, 6th century. Museo Archivescovile, Ravenna, Italy.

In western Europe a small residue of the Classical skills and learning was kept alive mainly within the establishments of the Christian Church. Early medieval furniture, what little there was of it, was clumsy and crudely built of thick timbers that were hewn with an adze rather than cut with a saw. Ornament tended to be haphazard and often bore little relation in scale to the object it was decorating. Decoration became heavily dependent on Romanesque architectural motifs such as columns and arcades, and similarly the chip-carved patterns usually imitated those invented first by the stonemason. The art of turning had been practised since Classical times, and turned decoration appears frequently on medieval furniture. Indeed in Cologne, the turners were a well enough established group to have formed their own guild as early as 1180. Painted decoration on furniture was very common, being cheap and colourful and relatively easy to execute.

During the Middle Ages in Western Europe, the kings, magnates and prelates who comprised the property-owning section of the population, were continually on the move as they travelled from one bleak, sparsely furnished palace or castle to another, taking with them all the furniture required to satisfy their very modest demands for domestic comfort. Such furniture was therefore limited to pieces which were transportable by waggon and pack-animal. The only element of luxury was provided by textiles, splendid and colourful tapestries to hang over the bare walls, carpets to cover the rough trestle tables, curtains and cushions.

The chest was by far the most common and practical piece of furniture made throughout the Middle Ages. Not only was it used for storing all kinds of goods and personal belongings but it could also function as a seat, bed or table. From an

*The Birth of the Virgin* by the Master of the Life of the Virgin, showing a 15th-century bed with its hangings looped up into bundles, a carved chest and a dresser. Alte Pinakothek, Munich.

early date chests were used as safes; some have a slot in the lid for collecting money, while many examples have heavy iron straps and locks. Bands of wrought iron served a dual purpose, for apart from strengthening and securing the chest they often provided the main decorative feature, as in the 13th-century French example probably made to contain church muniments. In 1287 the Synod of Exeter ordered that every church be provided with a chest in which could be stored books and vestments, and indeed most of the earliest chests that have survived are of ecclesiastical origin.

The folding stool was well adapted for medieval travel and, with its distinguished ancestry dating back through Classical times to Dynastic Egypt, it continued to be regarded as an appropriate seat for kings. Such status stools were often decorated with precious metals and stones or richly carved like the so-called Stool of St Ramon which dates from the 12th century. Numerous three- and four-legged stools were made, and benches, either free-standing or fixed to the wall, were also very common. The X-frame chair evolved from the folding stool but became heavier and no longer collapsible. Other chairs had solid backs and were often brightly painted.

Beds became increasingly important, but the hangings, which were suspended from rods or hooks in the wall, were usually considered of more value than the woodwork. Small folding or 'trussing' beds were popular, while beds of box-like form, sometimes built into special recesses, were made all over northern Europe as late as the 17th century and have survived particularly well in Scandinavia.

By the end of the 13th century furni-

Oak chest with chip-carved decoration. English, 13th century. Victoria and Albert Museum, London.

Chest covered with wrought iron scrollwork. French, 13th century. Musée Carnavalet, Paris.

15

ture design was reflecting the tracery, cusps, pointed arches and trefoils so typical of the Gothic style of architecture which was now firmly established in most parts of Europe. In spite of the fact that Gothic architecture evolved certain national differences, any attempt to place furniture into regional schools at this date must remain tentative, for it was not until the end of the Middle Ages that furniture began to display distinctive national features. Until then, all that can be said is that generally in northern Europe, where hard woods, especially oak, were preferred for furniture, deeply cut sculptural decoration was more favoured than in southern Europe where softer woods were less suitable for high relief ornament.

Gradually during the course of the 14th century social changes took place that were to affect greatly the development of furniture. The land-owning nobility began to enjoy a more settled existence, preferring to concentrate their wealth on one estate rather than several scattered over a wide area. This period also witnessed the rise of the merchant class, who had both the inclination and the money to spend on furnishings. Separate rooms, smaller and less public than the great hall, began to proliferate, and the bed-chamber became particularly significant. The curtains were still regarded as the most important feature of the bed, but by the end of the 15th century they were more often suspended from the full or half tester surmounting

The so-called Stool of St Ramon. 12th century. Cathedral of Roda de Isabeña, Huesca, Spain.

14

the bed, rather than from the wall or ceiling. The bed-chamber was also a reception room of major importance, and during the day, in order that the bed might also serve as a seat, the hangings were scooped up into bundles. The truckle bed, so often listed in contemporary inventories, was a low, lightweight cot, that was especially suitable for servants—who often slept in the same rooms as their masters—as it could be easily stowed under the great bed in the daytime.

Throughout this period stools and benches continued to be made in quantity, but the chair retained its throne-like connotations and was reserved only for those of great importance such as the master of the house. One of the most historic extant medieval chairs is the Coronation Chair in Westminster Abbey. This was made by Master Walter of Durham to hold the Stone of Scone brought by Edward I from Scotland, and the inspiration for its gabled back and arcaded sides is very obviously architectural. Another article indicating great prestige was the canopy made either of textile or of wood and erected only over those of the highest rank.

In the earlier Middle Ages one piece of furniture usually fulfilled several different functions, but by the end of the 15th century furniture had become more specialised, and new forms were appearing, such as the buffet. At first this was merely a stand of open shelves on which plate or other objects of value could be displayed, but by the end of the century it was often a substantial and important piece consisting of both shelves and closed compartments. Another new form was the livery cupboard, which was made to contain food and for this reason had pierced tracery on the doors in order to ventilate the contents. The cupboard became a more familiar article of furniture, and while even in the highest society meals were still served from trestle tables, dormant tables of more sophisticated construction now began to appear.

Chest carved with Gothic tracery. French, late 15th century. Victoria and Albert Museum, London.

*left*
Livery cupboard. English, late 15th century. Victoria and Albert Museum, London.

The Coronation Chair in Westminster Abbey, made by Master Walter of Durham to hold the Stone of Scone brought to England by Edward I in 1296.

# The Renaissance: Italy, France and Spain

## Italy

*about 1400–about 1560*

It is arguable that cassoni or marriage chests form the greatest single Italian contribution to the history of furniture, for those of superior quality were decorated by the finest artists of the day such as Botticelli, Donatello and Pollaiuolo, their subjects being by no means confined to marital and romantic themes. Cassoni often took the form of Classical sarcophagi; some were made of wood decorated with gilt gesso and carved with Classical motifs in light relief while others displayed intarsia panels of great beauty. In the painting and decoration of cassoni can be traced the transition from the medieval to Renaissance conceptions of ornament and form, and after about AD 1400 painted decoration on Tuscan examples evolved from small panels of two-dimensional patterning to more ambitious compositions such as can be seen on the early 15th-century 20 Florentine cassone illustrating the meeting of King Solomon and the Queen of Sheba. Although the figures are still elegantly Gothic in their stance and the style of their dress, the architecture depicted shows a new understanding of Classical order and perspective.

Intarsia, the name given to a type of pictorial inlay, was a medium in which Italian craftsmen excelled. Superb examples of this form of decoration are to be seen not only on cassoni but also on choir stalls and cupboards, such as that 19 dated 1502 with intarsia panels of landscapes and trompe-l'oeil still-life compositions. It was made for a monastic library and possibly executed by Fra Giovanni da Verona, recognised even by his contemporaries as the foremost intarsia artist of his day.

A plain type of seat known as a cassapanca was formed simply by adding two sides and a back to a cassone, but during the 16th century more elaborate chairs and stools also developed. Some were profusely carved with elegantly

18

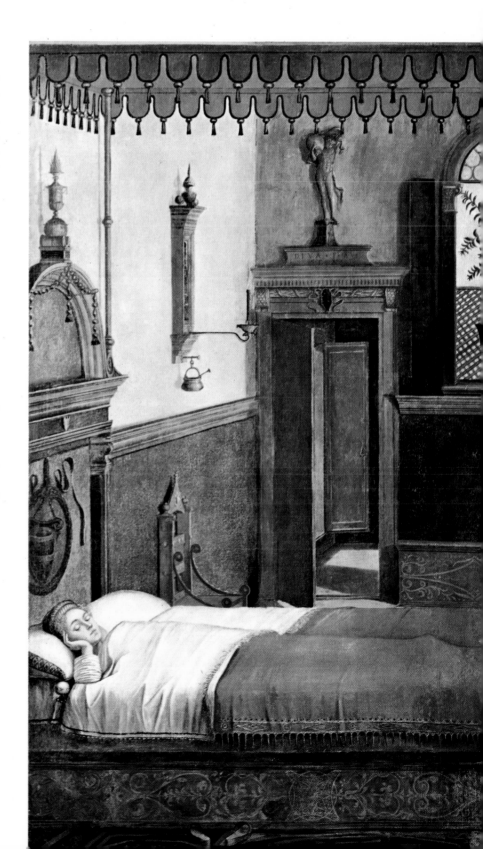

shaped profiles, while others were up-holstered, their uprights terminating in knob finials.

The supports of tables frequently recall forms drawn from Classical Rome, and although generally carved in wood, some of the grandest examples were sculpted in marble. An article of furniture that readily lent itself to architectural treatment was the credenza or sideboard which in the 16th century developed from a rough table into a piece of considerable magnificence.

During the 16th century there developed a fashion for highly carved and polished furniture which was neither gilded nor painted, but enjoyed for the colour of the natural wood. In the course of the century the style of carving underwent considerable changes. After the Sack of Rome in 1527, when the High Renaissance had passed its zenith, artists and designers began to break the well established Classical rules of clarity, scale and perspective with crowded compositions of contorted figures, attenuated sphinxes and abundant foliage. This Mannerist style of ornament is well illustrated by a pair of bellows carved 20 with grotesque masks surrounded by a scrolling frame.

The furniture with which the great Italian palazzi were equipped matched 21 in artistry the frescoes, carving, gilding and textiles which made their interiors so splendid, but the purpose of this furniture was more to delight the eye and stimulate the imagination than to provide soft domestic comfort.

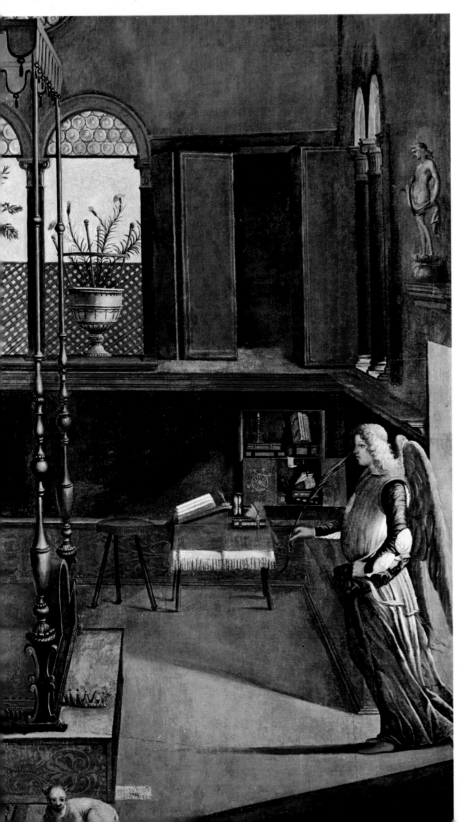

*The Dream of St Ursula* by Vittorio Carpaccio (about 1495) shows a typical sparsely furnished bed-chamber of a 15th-century Venetian palace. Accademia, Venice.

Cupboard decorated with intarsia, possibly by Fra Giovanni da Verona. 1502. Abbazia di Monte Oliveto Maggiore, near Siena.

# France

## about 1500–about 1600

The series of incursions into Italy by French invading armies under Charles VIII, Louis XII and Francis I retarded the remarkable advance of civilisation in northern Italy, but they also accelerated the spread of Renaissance ideas, tastes and art forms in France. These new influences on French furniture were at first quite superficial, Renaissance ornament being simply grafted on to medieval forms, but by the time that Francis I began the construction of the great palace of Fontainebleau, French craftsmen and designers had become broadly familiar with the whole vocabulary of the Italian Renaissance, largely through the work of a number of distinguished Italian artists, Leonardo da Vinci among them, who had chosen or been persuaded to bring their skills to France.

Among the most influential artists to work at Fontainebleau were Rosso and Primaticcio whose decorative schemes for the Long Gallery were to have a profound effect on contemporary French artistic thought. Instead of Gothic vaulting, pointed arches and quatrefoils the gallery is filled with frescoes executed in the Italian manner and surrounded with a complex framework of cartouches, cupids, garlands of flowers and a type of scrolling strap-like decoration that was to become such a feature of northern European ornament in the latter half of the 16th and early 17th centuries.

The status of furniture as an applied art rose dramatically during the 16th century, and the leading architects now began to concern themselves with its design. After the death of Francis I in 1547, architects such as Philibert Delorme, Pierre Lescot and Jacques Androuet Ducerceau, although fully aware of the Italian tradition, began to evolve a style more specifically French in character. Ducerceau was especially important as far as furniture is concerned for in 1550 he published a collection of engraved designs including many different types of furniture which were to have an influence reaching far beyond the borders of France. A dresser dating from about 1580 shows features typical of Ducerceau's individual approach. Although the motifs are largely based on classical examples, the treatment of the chimerae carved at the corners with scrolling tails and paw feet, together with the strapwork cartouches and the caryatids, illustrate the French Mannerist style at its most accomplished.

The dresser, a descendant of the buffet, usually consisted of an upper stage with closed compartments and sometimes several drawers, supported on either a stand formed of columns or a solid base with doors. Unlike the medieval buffet which was primarily a vehicle for displaying *objets de virtu*, the dresser was itself often elaborately carved or inlaid with precious materials.

Tables of simple trestle form continued to be made in the 16th century, but there also developed a more architectural type similar in conception to Italian examples

23

Pair of bellows, carved with Mannerist ornament. Italian, about 1550. Wallace Collection, London.

Painted panel of a 15th-century Italian cassone depicting the meeting of King Solomon and the Queen of Sheba. Victoria and Albert Museum, London.

with the end supports composed of carved caryatids, rams, eagles and foliage. Sometimes the supports were connected by an arcade of Classical columns resting on a thick heavy stretcher. Hugues Sambin, another Mannerist architect working at Dijon, who, unlike Ducerceau, actually practised as a cabinetmaker, produced some fine designs of such tables. The friezes were frequently decorated with Classical ornament, and many table tops had extending leaves. Round and square tables with a single central support were also made but were less common.

Both Ducerceau and Sambin produced designs for beds, and it can be seen from these and from other contemporary illustrations that, although the hangings were still immensely expensive, the wooden framework of the bed with its lavishly carved canopy, posts, headboard and base was now providing considerable competition as a decorative element.

The chest which had been such an essential article of furniture in medieval life was now declining in importance,

Bedroom in the Palazzo Davanzati, Florence. The furniture is 16th-century, but the mural decoration dates from the 15th century and is typically Tuscan in character.

but the cabinet, made to contain objects of intrinsic or sentimental value, was at an early stage in its evolution. The wardrobe or armoire, with one large door often flanked by columns, had appeared by the end of the 16th century, while Dijon became the centre for the production of a type of cupboard in two stages, known as an armoire à deux corps.

The role of women in society became more prominent during the Renaissance period. One instance of this increasing female influence was a chair, called a caquetoire, designed with a seat made wider at the front than at the back in order to accommodate the wide skirts of the period. Belonging to this same class of lightly built seat was an armless chair, then described as a back stool, and the tabouret, consisting of a large soft cushion supported on a low frame.

21

# Spain

## *about 1500–about 1600*

During the 16th century Spain rose to become the most powerful nation in Europe, and it was in this period of greatness that the finest Spanish furniture was made. As in France there was a transitional period between the Gothic and Renaissance styles, during which the new Classical motifs were applied to medieval forms. In Spain the earliest phase of the Renaissance is known as Plateresque (from *platero*, silversmith)

because Classical ornament was first applied to silver, and the intricate techniques of the silversmiths were later reflected in the carving of wood and stone. Plateresque carving became increasingly elaborate and exuberant until toward the end of the century it gave way to a more austere, but at the same time more italianate, Classical tradition that was better suited to the personal tastes of Philip II. It became known as Herreran after the name of its chief exponent, the architect Juan de Herrera.

Many of the same general trends took place in Spain in the 16th century as

This armoire à deux corps is typical of the cupboards made in Dijon in the latter half of the 16th century and is elaborately carved in high relief with Mannerist ornament. Philadelphia Museum of Art.

elsewhere in Europe. For instance, chests became less numerous, bed curtains now hung from the bed frame and the production of chairs increased in quantity and in the variety of styles. But Spanish furniture design was subject also to Arab influence, and a decorative style called 'Mudéjar', which was a fusion of Moslem and Christian art, was much in evidence throughout the 16th century.

24 The X-frame chair, known in Spain as the sillón de cadera or hip-joint chair, was made from the 15th century, the framework often decorated with ivory inlay of Mudéjar design. These chairs were sometimes richly upholstered, such as one described in the inventory of the Duke of Albuquerque which was covered in green velvet trimmed with a twisted silk fringe fastened by gilded nails.

By the middle of the century the hip-joint chair was being superseded by the sillón de fraileros or monk's chair. At its simplest this consisted of a rectangular frame of beech, walnut or orange-wood, hung with leather. Leather was a very characteristic feature of Spanish furniture, and a technique of working a raised pattern, often of heraldic design, was

Richly carved Spanish writing-cabinet. About 1650. Museo Sta Cruz, Toledo.

Dresser reflecting the influence of the French Mannerist designer, J. A. Ducerceau. About 1580. Frick Collection, New York.

Hip joint chair inlaid with Mudéjar decoration. First half of the 16th century. Museo de Artes Decorativas, Madrid.

Engraving of Henri II on his death-bed from *Guerres, Massacres et Troubles . . .* by Perrissin et Tortorel, published in 1569–1570. Bibliothèque Nationale, Paris.

known as guadamecil and was originally a speciality of Moorish craftsmen. Earlier examples of the monk's chair were made to fold, but as upholstery became more firmly attached to the frame this was no longer possible.

The escritorio or, to use its more familiar 19th-century name, vargueño was one of the most important Spanish contributions to Renaissance furniture. It evolved from a type of small cabinet in which churches kept their vestments, and in its fully developed form consisted of a chest with a falling front that revealed a set of drawers. It was placed on either a panelled or a trestle stand. The earliest vargueños display fine Mudéjar decoration, but later examples, of which some of the best come from Catalonia, have beautiful boxwood reliefs, often set against a velvet ground, while others with coloured marquetry interiors reflect the influence of contemporary German cabinetmakers. Although richly decorated inside, vargueños generally had plain exteriors the sole ornamentation being the pierced metal hinges and nails.

Caquetoire. French, about 1550.
Museum of Decorative Art, Oslo.

Vargueño decorated with boxwood
reliefs. Probably from Catalonia, first
half of the 16th century. Victoria and
Albert Museum, London.

# The Renaissance in Northern Europe about 1500-about 1630

Carved dresser with both cupboards and drawers. Second half of the 16th century. Schloss Zeil, Allgäu.

The introduction of the Renaissance to northern Europe in the first decade of the 16th century was due, in part, to the influence of such great artists as Holbein, Dürer and Mabuse, but much more to the art of the engraver which enabled pattern books of designs to be distributed internationally. Although Italy was the source and inspiration for the new repertoire of Classical motifs, the way in which they were treated and expressed by north European Mannerist architects, craftsmen and designers was very unitalianate and highly individual.

Dürer, Mabuse and probably Holbein had visited Italy, and a number of northern European artists working around the turn of the 15th and 16th centuries now considered a sojourn there to be an important part of their artistic education. One of these, the sculptor and carver Peter Flötner, established himself in Nuremberg in 1522, and his designs for furniture, reliefs and architectural ornament did much to spread Renaissance ideas to German craftsmen. Heinrich Aldegrever and Hans Sebald Beham are among other distinguished artists and engravers whose work was imbued with the Classical style.

In Flanders and the Netherlands the work of such artists as Lucas van Leyden and Cornelis Floris fulfilled the same pioneering role as their German counterparts. Perhaps the most important designer from the point of view of the cabinetmaker was Hans Vredeman de Vries. Following the precedent of the Italian architect Serlio, whose *Fourth Book of Architecture* had been translated into Flemish in 1539, Vredeman de Vries published his own account and interpretation of the five Classical orders in about 1565. This and later designs published in collaboration with his son Paul were to have a considerable influence on north European furniture of the 16th century.

Indeed in England, knowledge of the Italian Renaissance was only to a very limited extent drawn directly from Italy and was largely dependent on pattern books of Mannerist designs published in the Low Countries which found their way to England in increasing numbers.

The Wrangelschrank cabinet made in Augsburg in 1566. Landesmuseum, Münster, Germany.

# Germany

In Germany there were marked differences between furniture produced in the more conservative north and that made in southern towns, particularly Augsburg and Nuremberg, where there was a more adventurous approach to new ideas and a less rigid guild system. A cabinetmaker and designer known by the initials H.S. appears to have spent part of his career in Augsburg and produced woodcuts of panelling, doors and cupboards that show he had a considerable mastery of the Renaissance style. A wooden chest dated 1551 bears his initials and consists of three panels designed with perspective architectural views divided by Ionic columns decorated with carved scrolls, foliage and animal heads in the Classical manner.

Such elaborate marquetry was a distinctive feature of German cabinetwork. One of the more famous examples is a 26 cabinet known as the Wrangelschrank because it was looted in the Thirty Years War by a Swedish commander Count Wrangel. It was made in Augsburg and is dated 1566. The doors open to reveal an astonishing feat of crafts- 28 manship: the interior cupboard is carved in boxwood with complex historical scenes separated by Classical alabaster columns, while the doors are covered in marquetry of an almost surrealistic nature combining sculptural strapwork creations, architectural ruins, monkeys and birds. The intarsia work is highly reminiscent of the designs of Lorenz Stoer who published a series of his woodcuts in 1567 under the title *Geometria et Perspectiva*.

In northern Germany the development of Renaissance furniture took a less flamboyant and less imaginative course. Often carved in solid wood, such pieces as cabinets and cupboards were generally plain and even austere in appearance. Cupboards had been made from an early date in southern Germany and were probably first formed by placing one chest upon another. This horizontal format was commonly maintained until the latter part of the 16th century when a larger hanging cupboard was developed, although in the north this did not appear until the following century. 26 Dressers developed into more substantial pieces in the early 17th century and, like so much of the finest German furniture, were decorated with elaborate marquetry.

In the important furniture-producing towns of Augsburg and Nuremberg a noticeable change in taste occurred in the early part of the 17th century when plain veneers were frequently preferred to the more extreme Mannerist marquetry designs. In spite of the move toward greater simplicity, it was at this period that the craftsmen of Augsburg were producing a distinctive type of cabinet which was to excite admiration all over Europe. Made to contain small objects of value and composed of such valued materials as ivory, ebony, tortoiseshell, silver and semi-precious stones, these cabinets represent at its most skilled the work not only of cabinetmakers but of craftsmen of many different media. A cabinet given to King 28 Gustavus Adolphus illustrates how an object still essentially classed as a piece of furniture could now be considered a true work of art.

28 *Queen Mary Tudor* by Antonio Moro (1554). In this portrait Queen Mary is seen sitting in a richly upholstered X-frame chair. Castle Ashby, Northamptonshire.

Cabinet mounted with semi-precious
stones given by the city of Augsburg to
King Gustavus Adolphus of Sweden in
1612. Upsala University, Sweden.

*right*
Detail of the Wrangelschrank cabinet
illustrating the intarsia decoration.

*far right*
Design for two beds by Hans Vredeman
de Vries, from *Différents Pourtraicts de
Menuiserie*, about 1580.

# The Low Countries

## *about 1500–about 1630*

Under the Dukes of Burgundy in the 15th century the leading cities of the Low Countries rivalled those of Italy in their wealth and in their cultural output. With the passing of the House of Burgundy the Low Countries were left without an aristocracy, and the principal patron of the arts became the rich burgher who expected good honest value from the artistic objects in which he invested his capital. The houses of the burghers lacked the grandeur of the great Italian palaces, but their interiors were designed for comfort and practicality, and much of the furniture made at this time displays craftsmanship of a high standard.

By the 17th century, Middelburg, capital of Zeeland, was established as an important centre of furniture-making. A characteristic piece is the Zeeland chest, made in two stages, with doors often framed by caryatid figures. Some are ornamented with geometric shapes which are probably Arabic in origin and introduced into the Netherlands from Spain. The beeldenkast, of similar form, was made in the Province of Holland and is remarkable for its carved figures which were produced by specialist carvers.

During the first half of the 17th

century Antwerp gained a reputation for a particularly splendid type of cabinet finely veneered in ebony and tortoiseshell, and with doors and drawers painted with themes chosen to accord with the client's taste. These cabinets were exported all over Europe, and many were made in the workshops of the Forchoudt family whose name is closely linked with their history.

Chairs made in the late 16th and early 17th centuries have a sturdy rectangular appearance, and some examples, such as those with leather upholstery fixed by brass nails or with carved double stretchers and arcaded backs, reflect Spanish and Italian influence.

The bed was a highly regarded piece of furniture. Included among the designs published by Hans Vredeman de 29 Vries in 1580 under the title *Différents Pourtraicts de Menuiserie* are some for beds of architectural character which have richly carved frames and headboards. They are obviously intended to stand in the centre of the bed-chamber, but another type of bed common at the period was built into the corner of a room, such as the example from Dor- 30 drecht dated 1626, which shows how the panelling of the bed forms an integral part of the room itself.

29

Oak bed from Dordrecht, dated 1626. Rijksmuseum, Amsterdam.

'Queen Elizabeth's Virginals'. This late 16th-century Italian instrument may have been decorated in England by immigrant foreign craftsmen; on a panel to the left is displayed the coat-of-arms borne by English monarchs from Henry IV to Elizabeth I. Victoria and Albert Museum, London.

The Great Bed of Ware, whose carved decoration reflects the influence of Flemish Mannerism. English, about 1580. Victoria and Albert Museum, London.

Beeldenkast or cabinet decorated with carved scenes. Northern Netherlands, about 1630. Rijksmuseum, Amsterdam.

# England
## *about 1500–about 1630*

The influence of Flemish Mannerism may be seen on the Great Bed of Ware 31 with its exuberantly carved caryatid figures and the elaborate inlay decorating the headboard. Apart from its exceptional size, this bed has many features typical of the great Tudor bed such as the bulbous vase-shaped supports, strapwork ornament and heavily panelled tester. There are still traces of paint on the carving, a reminder that much furniture of this period was brightly painted. The woods used were usually indigenous, the most common being oak.

Chests continued to be made in large numbers, but after 1500 were more frequently of panelled than solid wood construction. As craftsmen became more familiar with the Flemish pattern books and with the few examples of Italian work in the country, Renaissance motifs began to mingle with Gothic ornament, as can be seen on the panelling of about 1530 from Waltham Abbey, where

medieval monsters are carved alongside roundels containing portrait busts in the Classical manner.

By the end of the 16th century, joined chairs with rectangular frames, thick stretchers, panelled backs decorated with floral or chequered inlay and curved arms had replaced the earlier solidly built box-chair. At the same time upholstered chairs were becoming more common. An especially grand example of the X-frame chair, to be seen in a portrait of Queen Mary Tudor in 1554 by Antonio Moro, is covered in crimson velvet, fastened with brass studs and hung with gold fringes. By way of contrast, elaborately turned chairs with triangular seats display great skill on the part of the turner but little in the way of comfort.

The court cupboard is the counterpart of the French buffet and, as the name suggests, was originally a short stand of shelves on which cups and plate were displayed. While food was stored in livery cupboards, the term 'press', first recorded in Chaucer's *Miller's Tale* in 1386, describes a taller piece with shelves or hanging space.

The bulbous vase-shaped supports noted on the Great Bed of Ware were also common on draw-tables. These could be doubled in length by extending the lower leaves and by the middle of the 16th century were a familiar feature in both the great hall and in the more private rooms. Apart from these and the trestle table, smaller examples, sometimes made to fold, were used for many different purposes.

Desks in the modern sense of the word were yet to evolve, but paintings exist showing scholars standing up and writing on boxes with sloping lids. An example in the Victoria and Albert Museum, London, is decorated with Nonesuch inlay composed of architectural spires and domes. This particular form of inlay was used in the decoration of chests and was probably introduced to England from Germany. The term 'Nonesuch' arose from the 19th-century misconception that the pattern derived from the architecture of Henry VIII's palace of Nonesuch, pulled down in the 17th century.

During the first decades of the 17th century furniture did not undergo any dramatic changes, but the flowing plant forms and arabesques so much enjoyed by Elizabethan designers gave way to more abstract and stylised patterns. A few new pieces, such as the chest-of-drawers, were introduced, but it was not until after the restoration of Charles II in 1660 that the age of cabinetmaking as opposed to joinery was to begin in England.

Court cupboard made of bulletwood and satinwood and decorated with semi-precious stones. English, early 17th century. Victoria and Albert Museum, London.

Joined chair with panelled back, turned supports and scrolled arms. English, early 17th century. S. W. Wolsey Ltd, London.

The Long Gallery at Aston Hall,
Birmingham. The elaborate fireplace,
plaster ceiling, tapestries and furniture
shown here are fine examples of early
17th-century craftsmanship.

# The Baroque

## Italy
### *about 1600–about 1730*

By the latter half of the 17th century Italian furniture had assumed the flamboyant curving forms of Baroque architecture and sculpture. Indeed for some pieces and especially for the console- or side-table, which evolved at this period, sculpture is a more apt description than furniture. Twisting human figures, swirling scrolls, imperious eagles, playing putti and large ornamental shells, all boldly and curvaciously carved, are typical of the forms employed in these magnificent tables. The architect intended them to be an integral part of his interior scheme of decoration, and they perfectly complemented the elaborately carved and gilded mirrors and picture-frames that hung on the walls above. Although their heavy marble tops gave these tables some practical function their purpose was primarily ornamental and many fine examples are still to be seen in the great galleries of Italian palaces.

Andrea Brustolon was one of the most famous and talented of the sculptors to turn his attention to furniture. Some splendid examples of his work survive in Venice, where he spent much of his career, such as the suite of furniture carved for the Venier family now in the

Palazzo Rezzonico, which features several stands carved in the form of Negroes swathed in chains and supported on sea monsters, that are typical of his bold imaginative approach.

Many relatively small pieces of Venetian furniture were decorated in imitation of oriental lacquer with chinoiserie designs – a fashion perhaps stimulated by the Venetians' long history of contact with the East. It is probable that Venetian craftsmen produced work in pietre dure, but Florence was by far the most important centre for this technique of making patterns or pictorial designs with inlay of semi-precious stones such as lapis lazuli, jasper, agate and porphyry. The Opificio delle Pietre Dure was founded by Fernando I in 1599 and was to produce for the Medici family such exquisite pieces as the table top designed by Jacopo Ligozzi and Bernadino Poccetti and made between 1633 and 1649.

It was on the decoration of cabinets that perhaps the most skilled craftsmanship and expensive materials were lavished at this period. These had by the later 17th century evolved from relatively small caskets into architectural pieces with cornices and columns and were sometimes supported on stands in the form of human figures. Cabinets were often used for the display of exotic woods, ivory carvings or panels of pietre dure.

Side table of carved and gilded wood. Italian, about 1680. Palazzo Spada, Rome.

Pietre dure table top designed by Ligozzi and Poccetti and made at the Opificio delle Pietre Dure between 1633 and 1649. Museo dell'Opificio delle Pietre Dure, Florence.

Chairs were varied in style, but among the most familiar was a rectangular type with upholstered back and seat and scrolling arms, showing that the Italian preoccupation with magnificence and elaboration did not entirely preclude a concern for comfort.

Vase-stand of carved ebony and boxwood. Part of the suite of furniture made by Andrea Brustolon for the Palazzo Venier between 1684 and 1696. Palazzo Rezzonico, Venice.

# The Low Countries

*about 1650–about 1730*

The exuberance of the Baroque style coincided with a period of great prosperity in the Low Countries and is reflected in much of the furniture produced there in the 17th century. The fact that cabinetmaking techniques had made enormous advances since the previous century is illustrated in the beautifully matched veneers, floral marquetry and lively carving that characterises so much of the finest Netherlandish furniture of this period. However the more sober side of the Dutch character is seen in the popular arched cupboard decorated with applied mouldings of oak and ebony made in the Province of Holland, while the doored cupboard in two stages standing on bun feet was also common.

In contrast to this relatively plain decoration, a centre table of about 1670 has carving in a fleshy malleable style described as 'auricular' because of its resemblance to the human ear which was first introduced by the silversmith Paul van Vianen. Tables with bases composed of putti, garlands of flowers and legs sometimes in the form of caryatids were numerous and in a more italianate tradition.

The tortoiseshell and ebony cabinets for which Antwerp had become so famous continued to be produced and widely exported, but by the end of the 17th century cabinets were generally of plainer form, the cabinetmaker preferring to achieve his decorative effect with carefully chosen and cut veneers. Of the many fine marqueteurs, Pierre Golle and Jan van Mekeren deserve special mention. The former moved to Paris and became ébéniste to Louis XIV, while van Mekeren had an important workshop in Amsterdam where he produced brilliant panels of floral marquetry of astonishing virtuosity.

French fashions were becoming increasingly dominant in Europe towards the end of the century and were even more firmly established after the Revocation of the Edict of Nantes in 1685 when large numbers of skilled Huguenot

*The Linen Cupboard*, dated 1663, by Pieter de Hooch. The large two-door cupboard decorated with applied mouldings in the form of an arch are typical of the northern Netherlands. Rijksmuseum, Amsterdam.

Side-table carved in the auricular style.
Northern Netherlands, about 1670.
Rijksmuseum, Amsterdam.

Cabinet-on-stand made in Antwerp. Veneered in ebony and tortoiseshell and inset with marble panels painted with biblical scenes. About 1650. Rijksmuseum, Amsterdam.

craftsmen fled from France to escape persecution. Daniel Marot, one of the most distinguished of these artists, worked for William of Orange, and his published designs did much to spread the French approach to style and orna-<sub>39</sub>ment. His designs for state beds, with their sumptuous upholstery falling in Baroque loops and swags and thick luxuriant tassels, are superb creations. He was also responsible for introducing more movement into the design of chairs, and those with tall backs, sometimes filled with rich carving and with scrolling legs and stretchers, are particularly associated with his name.

Engraved design for a state bed by
Daniel Marot from *Second Livre
d'Appartements*, about 1700.

# France
## about 1650–about 1710

The most distinguished pieces of furniture to appear in France during the first half of the 17th century were the products of foreign artists, mostly Flemish 43 or Italian, who were working in the country under the successive patronage of Henry IV, Marie de Médicis, Cardinal Richelieu and, in the early part of Louis XIV's reign, his ministers Mazarin and Fouquet. For the native craftsmen this was a period of apprenticeship which was to come to splendid fruition when Louis XIV and his minister of finance Colbert deliberately nourished and directed the arts for the purpose of glorifying the monarch and of making France, already the richest and most populated nation in Europe, the supreme arbiter of taste in the cultural and artistic world.

To further this policy, Colbert in 1663 founded the Gobelins workshops which, under the brilliant direction of Charles 41 Le Brun, were to produce the whole 43 range of magnificent furnishings required to adorn and complement the royal palaces. Thus began the great age of the ébéniste, a name applied to high quality cabinetmakers since the Frenchman Jean Macé had introduced from Holland the art of veneering cheap woods with ebony during the Regency of Marie de Médicis.

One of the most famous ébénistes working for Louis XIV was André- 47 Charles Boulle whose virtuosity in combining tortoiseshell and brass, sometimes together with pewter and exotic woods, was rarely surpassed. For this reason his name has been used to describe all examples of this method of decoration regardless of their date or country of origin. The majesty of Boulle's furniture, 42 as seen in the great armoire made for the mistress of Philippe d'Orléans, matched perfectly the sumptuous decoration in the vast rooms and galleries of Versailles.

The foundation of the Compagnie des Indes in 1664 stimulated interest in Eastern art. Lacquer furniture of all kinds was much in demand, but most popular of all were cabinets for which special stands were made and which were often adorned with oriental pots. The cabinet, so much a feature of the earlier part of Louis XIV's reign, was toward the end of the century superseded by the chest-of-drawers which was at first described as a bureau and later as as a commode. The term 'bureau', and

Jewel-cabinet, decorated with panels of pietre dure and supported on caryatids representing the Four Seasons. About 1670. Musée de Strasbourg.

The Long Gallery of the Hôtel Lambert on the Ile St-Louis, built between 1645 and 1650 under the direction of Charles Le Brun.

more specifically 'bureau-Mazarin', came to mean a writing-table standing on eight legs with a knee-hole flanked by drawers. Bureaux-plats were large centre tables, also intended for writing purposes, and often decorated with boullework and, like other furniture of the period, with bronze or brass mounts in the form of female heads, sun-bursts, acanthus sprays or grotesque masks. As in Italy console-tables were made for ornamental purposes and, although carved in a rich manner with a wealth of foliage, shells and scrolls, nevertheless display a greater discipline and restraint in execution than their Italian equivalents. Table legs were often in the form of pierced attenuated balusters that have an especially French character.

Chairs were very diverse, but the gradual trend to greater comfort towards the end of the 17th century is seen in a superbly upholstered type with tall rectangular back, curving arms, carved baluster- or scroll-shaped legs joined by carved stretchers.

At this period a number of different kinds of bed emerged, such as the lit à la duchesse and the lit de l'ange which, with their elaborate Baroque canopies, tassels, fringes and heavy folds, may be regarded as being among the finest creations of the upholsterer.

The furniture thus briefly described was only one expression of the unsurpassed grandeur of the court of Versailles which, for the next century, all the arbitrary kings and princelings of Europe strove to emulate within – and beyond – their means.

Armoire or cupboard by André-Charles Boulle that belonged to the Marquise de Piré, mistress of Philippe d'Orléans. About 1690. Musée des Arts Décoratifs, Paris.

French side-table carved to harmonise with the panelling of the room for which it was made. About 1680. Hotel Lauzun, Paris.

Bureau-plat or writing-table, attributed
to A.-C. Boulle. About 1710–1715.
Louvre, Paris.

Writing-desk by Domenico Cucci, one
of the highly skilled foreign craftsmen
attached to the Gobelins factory. About
1670. Collection of Mme Lopez
Willshaw, Paris.

# England
## about 1660–about 1730

The restoration of Charles II in 1660 brought a mood of national optimism that was to be strongly reflected in the decorative arts of the period. After the sanctimonious austerities of the Commonwealth, the aristocracy of England were now prepared to spend money on luxuries and furnishings on an unprecedented scale.

The Duchess of Lauderdale certainly spared no expense when she embarked on the redecoration of Ham House in the 1670s, and here the influence of contemporary French and Dutch fashions is much in evidence. Vivid colour is introduced everywhere, in the plasterwork, carvings and furniture and especially in the upholstery and wall-hangings. Vigorously carved chairs, their frames gilded, silvered or stained black to simulate ebony, are covered with scarlet and yellow silks and velvets and elaborate fringes. A contemporary inventory describes wall-hangings of 'crimson and gold stuff bordered with green gold and silver stuff' and 'blew damusk', and there were others of brocaded and yellow satin. In the dining room at Ham House, where the walls are hung in the Dutch manner with panels of stamped leather, can be seen a number of cane chairs with tall backs, twist-turned (or 'barley sugar') uprights and richly carved frames and stretchers. These became popular in the later 1660s when, after the Great Fire of London, there was a demand for relatively cheap but highly carved furniture.

Lacquer was greatly valued, but supplies imported from China by the East India Company could not meet the demand. It was therefore necessary to find a cheaper imitation that could achieve the same exotic effect. The term 'japan', although often used to describe oriental lacquer, in fact should refer only to its European imitation. In 1688 John Stalker and George Parker published a *Treatise on Japanning* which not only explained to the aspiring amateur and professional japanner how to prepare the necessary varnishes but also provided chinoiserie designs for them to copy. Japanned and lacquer cabinets were placed on stands that were sometimes crudely carved in the naturalistic Dutch manner with pot-bellied putti surrounded by leafy foliage while others were carved in the more sophisticated

The North Drawing-Room at Ham House, London. The plasterwork flanking the fireplace and the table and chairs date from the 1670s.

Bookcase with glazed doors, similar to those made for Samuel Pepys in about 1670. Victoria and Albert Museum, London.

Richly carved armchair with caned seat and back. About 1680. The Burrell Collection, Glasgow Art Gallery and Museum.

Japanned writing-cabinet by Martin
Schnell. About 1730. Museum für
Kunsthandwerk, Frankfurt.

French tradition with baluster supports and swags of fruit and flowers.

Flamboyant floral marquetry was introduced from Holland and used by English craftsmen to decorate tables, boxes, cabinets and longcase clocks. Subtle shading effects were achieved by dipping small pieces of wood into hot sand, while leaves were made of ivory stained green. Towards the end of the 17th century, oyster veneers, formed of cross-sections of roots and small branches, were in fashion and often seen in combination with floral marquetry.

Among new pieces of furniture to emerge during the Restoration period was the glazed bookcase of which the earliest known examples were made for Samuel Pepys by 'Simpson the Joiner' who earns several mentions in Pepys's famous diaries. Although these bookcases were obviously constructed by a joiner rather than a cabinetmaker, their quality and elegant proportions show Simpson to have been a craftsman of great skill.

Popular at this time were sets of furniture consisting of a rectangular table that stood under a mirror flanked by two candle stands. Such sets were generally decorated with marquetry or plain veneer, but some were completely covered with plates of embossed and

A set of silver furniture bearing the crown and cypher of Charles II and presented to the King by the City of London in about 1670. Royal Collection.

One of a pair of commodes made by A.-C. Boulle for the Trianon at Versailles. 1708–1709. Bibliothèque Mazarine, Paris.

47 chased silver. A substantial amount of silver furniture was in fact made, but little has survived because it was so often melted down in time of economic crisis.

Continental influence was greatly strengthened after the Revocation of the Edict of Nantes in 1685 and again with the accession of William III to the English throne in 1688. Among the many craftsmen and artists who followed William to London was Daniel Marot, whose work has already been referred to (see page 38) and whose influence on English furniture at the turn of the century was considerable. His French Baroque designs are reflected in a number of lavishly upholstered state beds made in England in the last decade of the 17th century. The bed-chambers in which great beds stood were usually furnished with a set of chairs formally arranged around the room and upholstered *en suite* with the bed hangings. Marot's name has been associated with the design of a type of chair produced in both Holland and England composed of a tall shaped back, carved splat and cabriole front legs. Early examples of the cabriole leg often terminate in hoof feet, but by the second quarter of the 18th century the claw-and-ball had become the most common foot used in conjunction with the cabriole.

In the last decades of the 17th century, there was a fashion for seaweed or endive marquetry consisting of finely cut sinuous scrolls and arabesques; but by the early 18th century marquetry had largely fallen from favour, and plain walnut
48 veneers were enjoyed for their warm colour and for the fine figure of the wood.

By this time English craftsmen had assimilated the new techniques and styles learned from foreign cabinet-makers and were producing chests-of-drawers, curving chairs with vase-shaped splats, knee-hole desks, card-tables and bureau-cabinets with scrolling pediments of pleasing design and very high quality. Such pieces were widely admired and influenced the furniture made in countries as far apart as Sweden, Italy and America.

The first two decades of the 18th century are primarily associated with finely proportioned walnut furniture, but there emerged in the 1720s a group of architects under the leadership of Lord Burlington whose influence was to inspire furniture of a very different nature. Their aim was to revive the Classical style as exemplified in the work

Bureau-cabinet veneered in walnut. The hooded pediments and bun feet reflect Dutch influence. About 1710. Private collection.

The Great Chamber at Chatsworth, built
and decorated in the 1690s. The
furniture is typical of the Palladian style
of the 1720s.

of the 16th-century Italian architect Palladio, and for this reason they became known as the Palladian school. Some of these architects, William Kent, Henry Flitcroft and John Vardy among them, also designed the furniture for the great country houses which they built. Having no originals on which to base their designs, they expressed their Classical tastes by fusing monumental architectural features such as massive consoles, Vitruvian scrolls and heavy cornices with the contemporary Italian Baroque style. Much of this Palladian furniture was decorated with gesso and was either left plain to resemble marble or stone or more often richly gilded. Furniture conceived on this grand scale was suited only to houses of palatial dimensions. Fine examples can be seen at Houghton and Holkham where the opulent Baroque interior decoration presents a remarkable contrast with the strictly Classical exteriors.

# Germany

*about 1650–about 1720*

After the devastation caused by the Thirty Years War, the second half of the 17th century in Germany witnessed an outburst of creativity. In the south, where Munich had now become both the cultural and the political capital of Bavaria, the Baroque style introduced from northern Italy was received with great enthusiasm, and palaces were filled with opulent furniture that matched in splendour their profuse plasterwork, boiseries and painted ceilings.

The influence of the auricular style is seen in the carved ornament of such characteristically German pieces as the large two-doored cupboards, so massive that only the hall could accommodate them. The published designs of Friedrich Unteutsch did much to spread this fleshy boneless style of ornament which is also frequently seen on chairs of the period. In their form, however, chairs were often modelled on 16th-century Italian prototypes.

The traditional German skill in the execution of wooden inlay is seen in a specialised type of decoration much used on cabinets and boxes, consisting of panels of intarsia carved in relief with mythological or biblical scenes. Pieces decorated in this manner are known as Egerware, after the small Bohemian city

Japanned cabinet on a silver-gilt stand. About 1685. The Vyne, Hampshire.

The Throne Room at the Royal Palace, Madrid, which is furnished with a splendid series of carved gilt pier-glasses and console-tables. About 1760.

Carved and gilt console-table designed by Henry Flitcroft. About 1735. Temple Newsam House, Leeds.

of Eger, which was the centre of their production.

In common with rest of Europe, German artists and designers in the latter half of the century turned to France for inspiration. H. D. Sommer was just one cabinetmaker working in the French manner and at his workshops in Künzelsau, Swabia, in the 1660s and 1670s was producing marquetry decoration of mother-of-pearl, horn and pewter of such quality that it would seem he must have learned the art in Paris.

# Spain and Portugal
## about 1650–about 1730

In spite of Spain's declining fortunes in the 17th century, expensive furniture continued to be in demand. Vargueños became even more numerous than in the 16th century, and another form of cabinet, the papelera, was decorated in ebony, ivory and tortoiseshell veneers. It stood on twist-turned legs and was surmounted by a pierced gallery. The Spanish and Portuguese taste for fancifully turned decoration is seen in many of the beds of the period on which the hangings now played a less important role. Chairs were in much wider use, and the monk's chair was modified to provide greater comfort. From the middle of the century, many chairs show strong French influence, while another type introduced from Portugal has a tall shaped back, brass finials and a particularly wide stretcher carved with scrolling designs.

Portugal broke free of Spanish rule in 1640, and her recovery of national pride is reflected in the furniture made there at this period, much of which is highly original. From her colonial territories, Portugal imported such exotic woods as jacaranda and pausanto · which were used in the construction of typically Portuguese chairs with arched back, turned supports and ball feet and covered with the highly embossed leather for which Portugal is justly famous. The contador is a cabinet similar to the papelera, but the geometrically shaped panels surrounded by wave mouldings show the influence of Holland.

From an early date Portugal established trade with the East, and evidence of this is seen in the many fine survivals of lacquer furniture.

52

Chair with turned supports, ball feet and embossed leather upholstery.
Portuguese, late 17th century. Museu Nacional de Arte Antiga, Lisbon.

State bed in the Queen Anne Room at Dyrham Park, Gloucestershire. Early 18th century.

# The Rococo

## France

### about 1710–about 1760

Although the name of André-Charles Boulle is closely linked with the Baroque monumentality of Louis XIV furniture, some of his later pieces are lighter and more curvacious, and their marquetry decoration reflects the style of the designer Jean Berain. Berain developed an individual style of ornament combining monkeys, tight-rope walkers, swings and arabesques that was largely inspired by the Classical grotesque – a whimsical type of ornament rediscovered on the walls of ancient Roman villas in the 16th century and used by such notable Italian artists as Raphael.

This more flexible approach to design gathered momentum during the Regency of Philippe d'Orléans (1715–1723) and in the furniture of the period is best reflected in the work of Charles Cressent who became ébéniste to the Regent. Cressent preferred to cast his own gilt bronze (ormolu) mounts although this was a flagrant breach of the guild regulations which strictly forbade one craftsman to practise the craft of another. Cressent's superb sculptural mounts are, however, a renowned feature of his richly veneered furniture, the commode and bureau-plat being characteristic examples.

The seeds of innovation planted in this transitional Régence period by Berain, Cressent and such architects as G. M. Oppenord and Robert de Cotte were to flower in the Rococo style which dominated the reign of Louis XV. The designers Nicolas Pineau and Juste-Aurèle Meissonier were two of the earliest exponents of the Rococo which, with its asymmetrical curving forms, organic nature and aura of gay abandon, was in conception a complete revolt from the severe Classical Baroque of Louis XIV. Included in the Rococo repertoire of ornament are such motifs as fantastic rock-like formations, plant forms from which animals and strange birds emerge, C-scrolls, human masks and amorphous cartouches, all intermingling in a care-free riotous manner.

Among the most brilliant ébénistes working at this period were Jacques Dubois, J. F. Oeben, his brother-in-law Roger Vandercruse (also called Lacroix) and Bernard van Risamburgh. Their furniture is generally decorated with floral or geometric marquetry and elaborate ormolu mounts, those to be seen on van Risamburgh's pieces being of exceptionally high quality. Both he and Dubois are also remembered for the production of particularly fine lacquer furniture. Madame de Pompadour, whose personal tastes have left an indelible stamp on the art of mid 18th-century France, shared with many others a passion for oriental objects, and to supplement the demand for lacquer furniture many pieces were decorated with the imitation, *vernis martin*.

Louis XV preferred the more intimate surroundings of the *petits appartements* in Versailles to the vast, draughty state rooms, and this did much to influence the evolution of furniture forms, now increasingly adapted to suit the new taste for comfort and informality. Comfort is the hallmark of the bergère, a deep wide chair with upholstered sides, back and seat and thick cushion, while informality is suggested by the names given to seats designed for two people such as the 'tête à tête' and the 'canapé à confidante'. Never before had there been so many different types of chairs designed for so many different purposes. Carved chairs were often intended to stand in a specific place within a room where the shaped back and carved decoration were made to match the

The Cabinet de la Pendule forms part of the *petits appartements* created for Louis XV at Versailles during the 1730s. The carving of the side-table reflects that of the boiseries behind.

Commode bearing the stamp 'B.V.R.B.' of Bernard van Risamburgh. About 1745. Rijksmuseum, Amsterdam.

Detail of a bureau-plat attributed to Cressent, showing the high quality of the ormolu mounts. About 1730. Louvre, Paris.

panelling of the wall behind. Beds too were generally designed to stand in a special position, and the popular lit à la polonaise was often contained in its own alcove. Tables, like chairs, were made in large numbers and varied greatly in shape and purpose. The encoignure, or corner cupboard, came into existence at this time and was surmounted with shelves, although these have rarely survived. The commode is in many ways the most familiar piece of the period and, with its bombé or serpentine shape, floral or geometric marquetry and magnificent ormulu mounts, is among the finest products of the Rococo style.

59

Bergère with deep, wide proportions and thick cushion. About 1750. Private collection.

Carved and gilt Rococo console-table. About 1740. Musée des Arts Décoratifs, Paris.

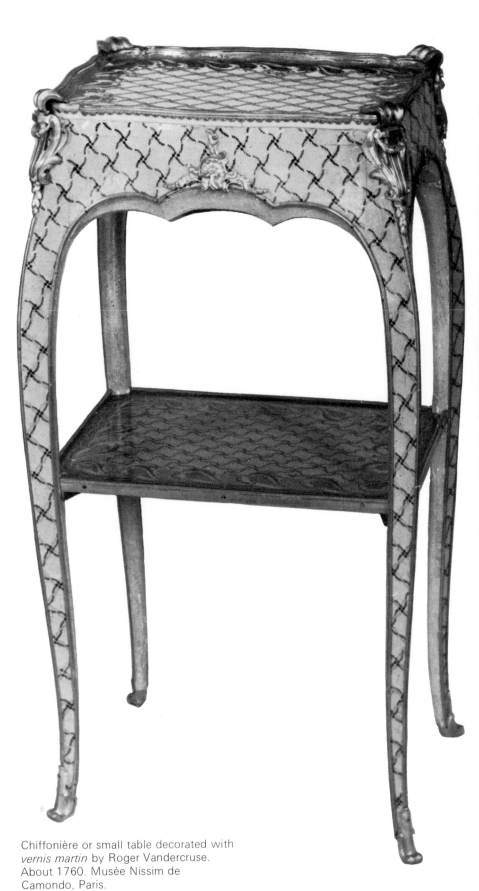

English side-table, made about 1740.
The design originates from an engraved
plate by Nicolas Pineau in his *Nouveaux
Dessins de Pieds de Tables* which was
plagiarised by Thomas Langley in his
*Treasury of Designs*. Victoria and
Albert Museum, London.

Chiffonière or small table decorated with
*vernis martin* by Roger Vandercruse.
About 1760. Musée Nissim de
Camondo, Paris.

# England

## *about 1730–about 1760*

During the 1730s and 1740s an increasing number of pattern books were published in England. These served a dual purpose for not only did they provide the craftsman with designs but also gave the potential client a catalogue from which to make his selection. One such book, the *City and Country Builder's and Workman's Treasury of Designs*, published by Thomas and Batty Langley in 1740, contains some twenty-five designs for furniture that are mostly Palladian in inspiration. However, the design of a side-table, [58] illustrated here, displays a very different tradition for it is directly copied from the French Rococo designer Nicolas Pineau. It is a complete contradiction of Palladian principles since it abandons Classical columns and architraves in favour of the sinuous curves and natural forms of the Rococo. As the designs of Meissonier and others found their way to England English craftsmen and designers became more familiar with the new style, but their own early essays in the Rococo were tentative and uncertain. The first craftsman-designer to handle Rococo ornament with real understanding and panache was Matthew Lock who in the 1740s published a series of designs for mirrors and tables (a splendid example of pier glass and console-table made in his workshop is preserved in the Victoria and Albert Museum).

Lock was responsible for engraving many of the plates in Thomas Chippendale's famous design book *The Gentleman and Cabinet-Maker's Director*. This book, which had three editions (1754, 1755 and 1762), played an important role in establishing the Rococo style in England. Apart from the originality of Chippendale's designs, the idea of producing a pattern book on such a large scale was also very new, and no cabinetmaker had attempted before to advertise his ideas and work in such a comprehensive manner. Because the designs contained in the *Director* could be imitated by any craftsman prepared to invest in a copy, Chippendale's fame has to some extent become distorted, for the number of high quality pieces known to have been made in his workshop are much less than the vast amount of furniture that has since been attributed to him. Unfortunately, English cabinetmakers, unlike the French ébénistes, rarely signed their work so that bills and inventories be-

Commode attributed to Cressent. About 1730. Rijksmuseum, Amsterdam.

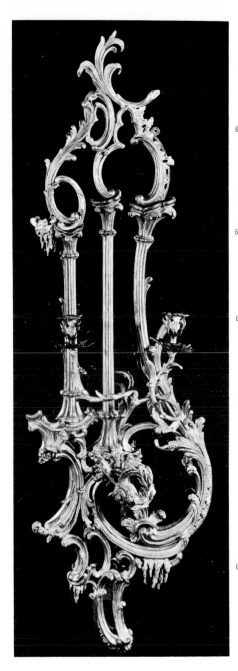

come vital in establishing the authorship of English furniture.

Typical of Chippendale's fresh approach to the design of furniture are chairs with pierced splats such as those composed of a ribbon motif. Chippendale himself describes them as 'ribband-back' chairs and goes on to say 'that if I may speak without vanity they are the best I have ever seen . . .' During this period a number of publications intended to rival Chippendale's *Director* were produced by the leading cabinet-makers, designers and craftsmen such as Thomas Johnson, the firm of Ince & Mayhew and Matthew Darly.

Chippendale's workshops were in St Martin's Lane, London, where most of the leading cabinetmakers, such as William Vile and John Cobb, William Hallett, John Linnell and Samuel Norman, also had their establishments and where there was situated Slaughter's coffee house, the meeting place of the keenest protagonists of the Rococo. William Vile was cabinetmaker to King George III and produced for him some superb pieces, such as a pair of medal-cabinets which, although basically Classical in form, are decorated with lively Rococo carving. They are made of mahogany which by now was the timber chiefly used for fine cabinet-furniture.

Apart from the 'French taste', the vogue for chinoiserie was an important facet of furniture design in the mid 18th century. Chippendale produced some fine japanned furniture for Badminton House and for the same house designed a 'Chinese' bed with pagoda canopy, red dragons and latticework headboard. Latticework was applied to all kinds of furniture – in the splats of chairs, around table-tops and on doors of cabinets.

Thomas Johnson, one of the most imaginative designers and carvers of this period, often included riotous collections of chinoiserie motifs in such pieces as mirror-frames and candle stands.

While the chinoiserie style was international, the mid 18th-century Gothic style was peculiar to England for, in spite of the Renaissance, medieval traditions had never been entirely forgotten by English designers. Chippendale produced some designs for 'Gothick' furniture, but in these Gothic ornament is usually applied to well established 18th-century forms such as the library desk or canopied bed which might equally well have been decorated with Rococo, Classical or chinoiserie ornament. Although at first sight it would seem that these styles have little in common, they all reflect the adventurous attitude to art current in the middle of the 18th century, and it is not uncommon to see all these traditions successfully mingled on one piece of furniture.

Carved and gilt girandole of about 1760, after plate 51 in Thomas Johnson's designs of 1758.

Japanned commode made in Chippendale's workshops for Badminton House, Gloucestershire, about 1754. Victoria and Albert Museum, London.

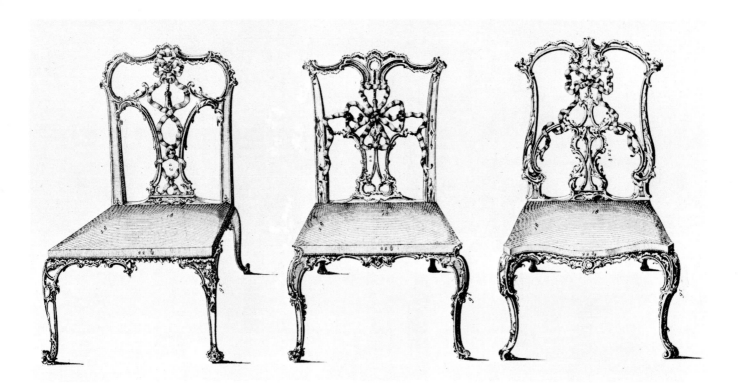

'Ribband-back' chairs, plate XV of Chippendale's *Gentleman and Cabinet-Maker's Director*, 1754.

Bedstead made by John Linnell for
Badminton House, Gloucestershire, after
a design in Thomas Chippendale's
*Director*. Mid 18th century. Victoria and
Albert Museum, London.

'Ribband-back' settee in the style of
Chippendale. About 1760. Victoria and
Albert Museum, London.

Design for a 'Gothick' bed, plate XXIX
of Chippendale's *Gentleman and
Cabinet-Maker's Director*, 1754.

Bureau du Roi. This magnificent piece was begun by J. F. Oeben for Louis XV in 1760 in the Rococo idiom but completed by his pupil J. H. Riesener in 1769 who was to become one of the leading exponents of the Neo-Classical furniture style. Versailles.

# Germany

## *about 1720–about 1760*

In the 18th century, the great palaces of Germany such as Pommersfelden, Würzburg and the Zwinger in Dresden were filled with furniture that, although of an unmistakeable German character, was often based on French prototypes, while in the north Dutch and English influences were also sometimes apparent. Because of the multiplicity of courts ruled over by electors, princes and bishops, marked regional differences developed in German furniture.

Mainz, for instance, was a noted centre for the production of cupboards and writing cabinets of curving form decorated with rich marquetry and carved volutes, while in cities like Aachen and Cologne oak furniture, carved with great sensitivity, has close French affinities.

Some of the finest Franconian 18th-century furniture was made for the Residenz in Würzburg where initially French craftsmen were employed but were later replaced by such distinguished cabinetmakers as K. M. Mattern and J. G. Nestfell, both highly skilled German marqueteurs, while the court sculptor, Johann Wolfgang von den Auvera, was responsible for some superb Rococo console-tables. Exuberant and imaginative carving is seen on a settee carved by the Spindler brothers, who later worked in Berlin but in the 1750s were established in Bayreuth which, together with Ansbach and Bamberg, was an important Franconian centre of furnituremaking.

In Georg Wenzeslaus von Knobelsdorff, Frederick the Great of Prussia found an able administrator to organise the redecoration of his palaces of Charlottenburg, Potsdam and Sanssouci. Knobelsdorff gathered a talented team of craftsmen, among them being J. A. Nahl whose seat furniture with its bold curving lines and vigorous carving represents some of the best early German Rococo. Nahl was succeeded at the post of Directeur des Ornements first by the Hoppenhaupt brothers and then by the Swiss J. M. Kambli who is particularly remembered for the splendid ormolu mounts that adorn his furniture and for the Bronzezimmer ('Bronze Room') in Frederick's palace in Berlin which was completed in 1755.

In Saxony French influence is seen in commodes which, although of rectangu-

lar form in the first decades of the 18th century, had by the 1740s adopted undulating curves. Seat furniture too, was mainly based on French models, but there was a fashion for English chairs of which a number were made by the court chairmaker J. P. Schotte. English originals also provided the basis for the design of Dresden cabinets. These were formed of two stages, with a writing bureau below and two doors with panels of mirror glass above, such as that made by Martin Schnell.

One of the finest expressions of the German Rococo, and indeed of the Rococo style anywhere, is to be seen in the decoration of the Nymphenburg 66 Palace and the Residenz in Munich. Here François Cuvilliés, who like the court architect Joseph Effner had studied in Paris, was responsible for much of the brilliant, daring interior decoration and for the sophisticated furniture such as the carved and gilt commode executed to his 65 design by J. A. Pichler in 1761.

Bureau-cabinet by K. M. Mattern of Würzburg in 1744. Mainfränkisches Museum, Würzburg.

Commode designed by François Cuvilliés for the Residenz, Munich, and executed by J. A. Pichler in 1761. Residenzmuseum, Munich.

Hall of Mirrors at the Amalienburg,
Schloss Nymphenburg, Munich. A
superb expression of the German
Rococo designed by F. Cuvilliés in
1734–1739.

Sofa made in 1764 by Johann Köhler of
Würzburg for the Residenz. Residenz,
Würzburg.

# Italy

## about 1730–about 1770

The 17th-century Italian taste for opulence and splendour which Baroque furniture successfully gratified continued undiminished into the middle years of the 18th century, and for this reason French Rococo made little headway in Italy except in Turin, where the most skilled Italian cabinetmakers were to be found, and in Venice, where the curving Rococo forms tended to be exaggerated sometimes to the point of absurdity. Some of best examples of Italian Rococo can be seen in the furniture of the Palazzo Caraglio, Turin, built during this period.

Sculptural furniture remained in vogue, and some splendid pieces were designed by the Venetian sculptor Antonio Corradini, notably a chair in the Palazzo Rezzonico, Venice, the framework of which is entirely composed of tumbling putti and mermaids.

If the rich Baroque furniture on display in the state rooms and galleries of Italian palaces remained little changed during this period, new and more practical furniture was being made for the smaller living rooms of palaces and for the houses of the prosperous bourgeoisie. North Italian 18th-century furniture is less sophisticated and less well constructed than the French, but its colourful, exuberant and often eccentric qualities have undoubted charm. Foreign fashions are reflected in much of the seat furniture, but the enormously long sofa or portegha was an Italian innovation designed for palace ballrooms. Dutch and English influences are seen especially clearly in the bureau-cabinet introduced during the first half of the 18th century. This generally consisted of a chest-of-drawers with a falling-front for writing on and a cupboard with a curving pediment forming the upper stage, but a bureau-cabinet made in 1738 for the Palazzo Reale in Turin is of a very different design. This was made by Pietro Piffetti, the most famous Italian cabinetmaker of the period, who also produced, often in collaboration with the architect Juvarra, some furniture remarkable for the extraordinary expertise and complexity of its marquetry decoration.

At this time lacquer and lacquer-imitation furniture was much in demand and was being made in many Italian cities, Venice being the most famous for this product. Venetian craftsmen de-

Steps and table with matching mirror and cupboard by Pietro Piffetti. 1731–1733. Palazzo Reale, Turin.

vised a particularly cheap method of giving an impression of lacquer decoration called 'lacca contrafatta'. This was a process of varnishing painted furniture which had been decorated with specially printed coloured paper cut-outs of chinoiserie designs. Another contemporary Italian contribution to the art of decoration was provided by Enrico Hugford who developed an improved method of painting on to scagliola (imitation marble). Hugford and his pupils produced in this medium panels and table tops of great beauty and subtlety. Unlike pietre dure which remained prohibitively expensive, painted scagliola became widely appreciated, and its popularity in England is testified by the many fine examples still to be seen there in great country houses.

# Spain and Portugal

## about 1730–about 1775

By the middle of the 18th century Spanish furniture had become more varied in type and lighter in construction. The elegant contours of the Rococo are seen in the carved gilt console-tables and matching mirrors that had recently been introduced from France. Mirrors were a particular feature of the Spanish interior, and in 1736 Philip V founded a royal factory for their production at San Ildefonso.

A blend of French Rococo styles and native traditions can be seen in a number of the chairs of this period which display cabriole legs joined by outmoded stretchers, curved backs that are too tall for the latest French fashion and upholstery of Spanish leather stamped with a French design. English influence was also very strong, and the simple curving forms, typical of the furniture made during the reigns of Queen Anne and George I, were widely copied but brought up to date with Rococo embellishments. Giles Grendey, a well known English cabinetmaker working in the first half of the 18th century, was especially concerned with the export of furniture to Spain, much of which was caned and decorated in red japan. Chairs were also made to Chippendale's designs, but their carved decoration is distinctly Spanish in character.

The Treaty of Methuen (1703) cemented the already well established links between Portugal and England and, although Portuguese architecture was mainly influenced by Italy and Austria, furniture styles were largely drawn from England. Some chairs are reminiscent of the Louis XIV period, others retained their tall back and leather upholstery in the old tradition, and occasionally chairs show a happy fusion of both French and English Rococo styles. Tables, cabinets and commodes were nearly always inspired by French, English or Dutch originals, but beds with their highly carved head boards and bold cabriole legs remained wholly Portuguese in character.

Portuguese bed with richly carved frame. About 1750. Collection of Russell de Sousa, Oporto.

# The Low Countries and Scandinavia

## about 1730–about 1760

In the 17th century Dutch cabinetmakers had made an appreciable contribution to the evolution of English and French furniture, but in the following century this position was reversed. For instance, cabinetmakers working in The Hague were required by the guilds to submit an 'English Cabinet' for their masterpiece. Chairs with cabriole legs and pierced splats, bureau-cabinets with glass panelled doors, and slender tea tables are of a strongly English character, whereas bombé commodes with floral marquetry and carved oak cupboards from Liège are closely related to French examples.

Scandinavian furniture of the 18th century is largely an amalgam of English and Dutch styles, although French influence was predominant in the high quality court furniture. A cabinet made in about 1751 by Mathias Ortmann, a cabinetmaker established in Copenhagen, is in the early 18th-century Anglo-Dutch style, but in an attempt to make it appear more fashionable a richly carved Rococo cartouche surmounts the pediment. The combination of early 18th-century forms with exaggerated Rococo decoration is well exem-

plified in chairs based on English 1730 models made in Norway and Denmark with curious lopsided Rococo carved ornaments.

The influence of the French Rococo was far more significant in Sweden, and a number of Swedish architects and craftsmen were sent to Paris to complete their training; but in Norway and Denmark German styles remained the strongest influence.

Cupboard carved with Rococo ornament made in or near Liège in about 1745. Musées Royaux d'Art et d'Histoire, Brussels.

# America
# about 1650-about 1790

## Jacobean

Although by the 1650s there were settlements of European immigrants along most of the eastern seaboard, the earliest survivals of American furniture were nearly all made in Massachusetts and Connecticut. In type, form and ornamentation they are so close to English early 17th-century examples that furniture made between 1650 and 1690 is generally described as 'Jacobean'. Early American furniture was primarily practical and functional, but such pieces as cupboards, writing boxes and chests could display vigorous carved decoration; and while popular strapwork motifs and foliated scrolls were obviously of Anglo-Dutch inspiration, the lively but curiously flat manner in which such ornament was treated is highly individual.

Numerous chests were made and, by the end of the century, were usually raised on short legs with one or two drawers forming the lower section. Hadley chests (named after a town in Massachusetts) were of this type, and their production is associated with a number of joiners among them John Allis and his son Ichabod, Samuel Belding and John Hawkes. They are carved in low relief with flowers and foliage and painted black, red, brown or green. Peter Blin is thought to have been responsible for a group of similar examples known as Hartford chests which are characteristically decorated with a
74 tulip and sunflower motif, oval bosses and applied spindles. The logical development of such chests was the chest-of-drawers, and a very early example with both painted and turned decoration is dated 1678.

Turned spindles are the chief decora-
73 tive feature of Brewster and Carver
70 chairs (thus named after two leaders of the early Massachusetts settlers) which with few exceptions have rush seats, while wainscot chairs are similar to the panelled-back English examples of some fifty years earlier. Joined stools and 'stretcher' tables were of simple rectangular form with turned supports and thick stretchers. Court cupboards and presses were the pieces invested with the most status, and these were embellished with geometric panels and a forest of spindles. The earliest extant beds are simple structures with low headboards and framework decorated with the inevitable turning, although it is obvious from contemporary inventories that more sophisticated high-post beds with canopies were known and highly regarded.

## William and Mary

The new techniques and fashions adopted by English craftsmen during the reigns of Charles II and William III were, after a time lag of some years, reflected in American furniture, and in the three decades 1690–1720, known as the William and Mary period, high quality furniture became the product of the cabinetmaker rather than the joiner. Towns such as New York, Charleston and particularly Newport and Philadelphia emerged to rival Boston as important centres of furniture-making.

The highboy (the term is 19th-century) was an important piece consisting of a finely veneered chest supported on a stand containing one or several drawers flanking a central open-

The Hart Room at the Winterthur Museum in which are shown a number of late 17th-century pieces which, with the exception of the gate-leg table, were all made in New England. A Carver chair stands by the fireplace. Henry Francis du Pont Winterthur Museum, Delaware.

ing and with turned legs linked by
76 curving stretchers. The term 'lowboy' describes such a stand which when separated from the chest became a dressing-table. In New York and the New Jersey area belongings were stored
77 in a kas, a cupboard based on the vast two-doored 17th-century Netherlands cupboards. The American version was painted with grisaille still-life paintings and could be easily dismantled.

The writing-box with sloping hinged lid was first placed on an open stand but later was more fashionably combined with the chest-of-drawers to form a slope-front desk.

The banister-back chair was a simpler variety of the elaborately carved English cane seats, but perhaps more familiar were the ladder-back chairs designed with horizontal slats of various shapes.

Caned day-beds made an appearance towards the end of the century as did the splendid upholstered easy chair with high back and protecting wings which continued to be popular in one form or another until the 19th century. An early 18th-century example illustrated in the 75 Index of American Design has rolling arms and cabriole legs terminating in paintbrush (also called Spanish) feet. Some elegant chairs with vase-shaped splats have been identified as the work of John Gaines, one of the few craftsmen to emerge from the general anonymity of furniture-makers of this period.

Tables were much more varied by this time, and a characteristically American version of the popular gate-leg table is the butterfly table, usually oval in shape with two folding wings and exaggerated splayed legs.

Couch made of maple with cane end and seat. New England, late 17th century. Metropolitan Museum of Art, New York (Gift of Mrs Russell Sage, 1909).

72

# Queen Anne

In England high quality furniture was invariably made in London; but in America, although cabinetmakers consistently followed English fashion, there were many individual variations on current themes, and throughout the 18th century regional differences are strongly apparent.

During the Queen Anne period (1720–about 1750) furniture made in Massachusetts is recognised for its tall slender proportions and pleasing elegance. Newport furniture is especially distinctive and is often made in the rich dark Santo Domingan mahogany. John Goddard, a founder member of the famous Townsend/Goddard family of cabinetmakers based in Newport, is associated with a form of claw-and-ball foot in which the ball is of oval shape and the claw undercut and pierced. Slim splats and flat serpentine stretchers are familiar features of Newport seat furniture but not exclusive to that town. In New York the original Dutch influence diminished, but furniture made there retained a strong square appearance with cabriole legs of somewhat heavy form. Among the finest chairs of the period were those made in Philadelphia. They are distinguished by their graceful outlines, vase-shaped splats and cabriole legs that terminate in web, pad or trifid feet. William Savery (active 1740–1787), one of the best-known Philadelphian furnituremakers, is chiefly remembered for his pieces in the Chippendale period, but he also produced some fine examples in the Queen Anne style.

The predominant curving line seen in furniture design during the early 18th century was a distinctive innovation, but otherwise surprisingly few new forms were introduced although many established ones were modified. The upholstered sofa did, however, make its first appearance at this time and, with its shaped back and rolled arms, rivalled the easy chair for comfort. Windsor chairs also came into existence in the middle of the century. The earliest examples have low rounded backs, but among the varieties that developed later were the low back, comb-back, fan-back and hoop-back.

Brewster-type armchair, made in Massachusetts in about 1650.
Metropolitan Museum of Art, New York
(gift of Mrs J. I. Blair, 1951).

A sunflower and tulip chest, with carved decoration. Late 17th century. Index of American Design.

The earliest known example of a chest-of-drawers, dated 1678. Henry Francis du Pont Winterthur Museum, Delaware.

An early 18th-century wing chair with rolled arms and paintbrush feet. Index of American Design.

75

The fact that folding card-tables, tea-tables, cupboards built into the wall, highboys and desks were all familiar in the well-to-do American house of this period illustrates what an enormous advance in prosperity and domestic comfort had been made since the days of the early settlers.

Turned and inlay decoration had by the 1730s given way to carved ornament, the shell being the favourite motif for the knee of the cabriole leg. Black walnut was the wood most commonly used, but butternut or white walnut is more often seen on country pieces. Maple is associated with New England and Pennsylvania, and cherry with Connecticut. Japanned decoration was advertised early in the 18th century in both Boston and New York, but it never achieved the same popularity as in Europe.

# Chippendale period

In spite of the Colonies' growing hostility to England which culminated in the Declaration of Independence in 1776, the latest English pattern books continued to be much in demand. The most influential of these was Chippen-dale's *Gentleman and Cabinet-Maker's Director*, and consequently the years between about 1755 and 1790 are described as the Chippendale period. The claw-and-ball was the foot most commonly used in conjunction with the cabriole leg, and splats of chairs were usually pierced with various designs which were largely based on those of Chippendale.

Philadelphia, by now the most flourishing city in America, was also the leading centre for the production of fine furniture and numbered among its cabinetmakers such renowned figures as Thomas Affleck, Benjamin Randolph, William Savery, Jonathan Gostelowe and Jonathan Shoemaker. One of the fine pieces attributed to Affleck, who worked for the Governor John Penn, is a rare mahogany side table with fret carving and Marlborough block feet. Perhaps the most splendid pieces produced in Philadelphia at this time were highboys. These were made in richly coloured mahogany with bold scrolling swan-necked pediments and were nearly eight feet tall. Benjamin Randolph's elaborately engraved trade card illustrates that he was familiar with a wide range of Rococo ornament which he handles with great skill on the set of six so-called

A painted kas, made in the New York area in the early 18th century. Metropolitan Museum of Art, New York (Rogers Fund, 1909).

Lowboy of walnut with turned supports and curving stretchers. About 1700. Collection of Colonel and Mrs Miodrag R. Blagojevich.

Block-fronted mahogany chest-on-chest attributed to members of the Goddard/Townsend family who were active in Newport, Rhode Island. About 1770. Henry Francis du Pont Winterthur Museum, Delaware.

Vauxhall Dining-Room at the Winterthur Museum in which are displayed some fine examples of Philadelphian chairs. About 1735. Henry Francis du Pont Winterthur Museum, Delaware.

sample chairs now divided between various American museums.

In Massachusetts furniture was still delicate and slender. The cabriole legs were particularly refined, and to provide extra strength the block-and-spindle stretcher was normally retained although it had generally fallen from fashion elsewhere. The claw-and-ball was characteristically carved with the side talon sharply turned back.

Block-front cabinets and desks were made in a number of towns, but some of the best examples were of Newport origin and produced by members of the Townsend/Goddard family. These pieces, usually made out of solid wood, have alternate concave and convex sections and display richly carved motifs. Block-fronts were also produced in Connecticut but were generally less sophisticated than the Newport examples. Carved sunbursts and fluted and chamfered corners are common features on Connecticut pieces.

New York cabinetmakers mostly resisted the curvacious forms of the Rococo style, preferring to retain squarer, heavier proportions in their furniture. However, occasionally a Gothic ogee can be detected in the splat of a chair, or a card-table is designed with a bold serpentine line. In the South, Charleston was the only city to produce good quality furniture on any scale. Thomas Elfe had a thriving workshop there and is known for applying fretwork to many of his pieces.

Pennsylvania Dutch describes furniture made by German-Swiss immigrants who had settled in Pennsylvania in the late 17th century. It has little to do with Chippendale but is characterised by lively colourful decoration. Christian Selzer of Jonestown, Dauphin County, made a number of the typically long rectangular chests painted with tulips, hearts, horsemen and such stern mottoes as 'Better be Dead than Faithless'.

The Commons Room at the Winterthur Museum showing a variety of Windsor chairs of the Queen Anne period. Henry Francis du Pont Winterthur Museum, Delaware.

78

# The Neo-Classical Age

## France

### *about 1760–about 1830*

In the middle of the 18th century the remarkable excavations at Pompeii and Herculaneum greatly stimulated the already reviving interest in the Classical arts just at a time when the taste for Rococo was beginning to wane. The engraver Charles Nicolas Cochin, the Comte de Caylus and the scholar Lalive de Jully were prominent among those who, during the 1750s, were effectively advocating the rejection of Rococo frivolities in favour of the purer principles of Antiquity, and although Louis XVI himself continued to patronise Rococo artists the Neo-Classical style steadily gained asendancy and was fully established before the king died in 1774.

The decade between 1760 and 1770 was a transitional period when the curving forms of furniture became less pronounced and its decoration more restrained. These features are exemplified in a roll-top desk of a type first
85 introduced by J. F. Oeben who had a reputation for the production of ingenious mechanical furniture.. In this piece of about 1765 the ormolu mounts are no longer lavishly spread over the surface but are of a more practical nature. The panels of floral marquetry are characteristic of Oeben's work and were often used in conjunction with designs of cubes, lozenges and rosettes. A fashion for pictorial marquetry developed around the middle of the century and was stimulated by a number of German craftsmen who operated in Paris at this time, many of whom were highly skilled marqueteurs. The most renowned of these cabinetmakers was David Roentgen whose furniture is decorated with superb panels of pictorial marquetry that display an astonishing painterly quality.

Oeben's pupil J. H. Riesener is generally regarded as being the most brilliant and versatile French ébéniste of the second half of the 18th century. His

Marie Antoinette's Boudoir, part of the *petits appartements* at Versailles. The writing-bureau and table are inlaid with mother-of-pearl. About 1780.

82

early pieces reflect the style of Oeben, but by about 1775 his marquetry designs become more geometric and are often composed of a lozenge or trellis pattern. In the 1780s Riesener's furniture was decorated less with marquetry and more often with plain mahogany veneer in the English manner. His output included the whole range of contemporary furniture from cabinets and commodes (now straight sided and often with projecting central sections) to work-tables, jewel-boxes, chiffonières and small writing-tables. Such pieces are also distinguished for the exquisite quality of their ormolu mounts, thought to have been the work of Pierre Gouthière, who was one of the foremost fondeurs-ciseleurs (workers

One of a pair of bonheurs-du-jour, decorated with Sèvres porcelain by Martin Carlin. About 1770.

Chiffonier bearing the stamp of J. F.
Oebén. About 1760. Louvre, Paris.

Work-table made by J. H. Riesener in 1788 for Queen Marie Antoinette. Musée de Nissim Camondo, Paris.

Roll-top desk attributed to J. F. Oeben. About 1765. Musée de Nissim Camondo, Paris.

of ormolu and bronze) of this period.

Furniture decorated with plaques of Sèvres porcelain became popular and a speciality of the dealers Poirier and Daguerre for whom the ébéniste Martin Carlin made a number of elegant pieces ornamented in this manner. Another method of introducing colour into furniture was by the use of red, green and blue *vernis martin* (imitation lacquer). Weisweiler, one of the German ébénistes to enjoy the patronage of Queen Marie Antoinette, decorated much of his furniture in this way but is also justly famous for his pieces veneered with finely figured wood adorned by ormolu mounts of exceptional quality. In the second half of the 18th century new types of multi-purpose furniture were developed such as the bonheur-du-jour which combined a dressing- and writing-table and the table à pupitre which served both as work-table and reading-desk.

New designs for chairs were published in the 1770s by Roubo and J. C. Delafosse that show straight tapering legs and curving frames decorated with swags and garlands. The most outstanding among the highly distinguished menuisiers working at this time was Georges Jacob. Jacob's inventiveness is seen in the enormous variety of chairs he produced between 1770 and the Revolution in 1789. Some examples have round, square or medallion-backs, others are of mahogany with carved and pierced splats, and some, such as the set made for Marie Antoinette's 'Dairy' at Rambouillet, are in the so-called 'Etruscan style' – a style using Etruscan and other Classical decorative elements which appeared shortly before the Revolution.

The turbulent years of the Revolution were, not surprisingly, unproductive of new designs, but under the comparative calm of the Directoire cabinetmaking began to revive. Directoire furniture is fundamentally in the Louis XVI tradition, with the Etruscan style dominant, but until the French economy began to prosper under Napoleon, there was little money available for lavish decoration. The more austere and academic approach to furniture design is seen in that depicted in the paintings of J. L. David, with its rectilinear profiles, sabre legs and plain surfaces. A number of ébénistes working under the Ancien Régime survived the upheaval of the Revolution, among them Georges Jacob who after the suppression of the guilds in 1791 was thenceforward able to practice both as a menuisier and an ébéniste. His workshop

85

The Grand Salon of about 1780 at the
Musée de Nissim Camondo. The
lacquer cabinet is by Weisweiler and the
round centre table decorated with
Sèvres porcelain by Martin Carlin. The
chairs are upholstered in tapestry and
are stamped by Georges Jacob.

Bedroom of the Empress Josephine at
Malmaison. The bed is signed by
Jacob-Desmalter, and the other pieces
shown here are similar to designs by
C. Percier.

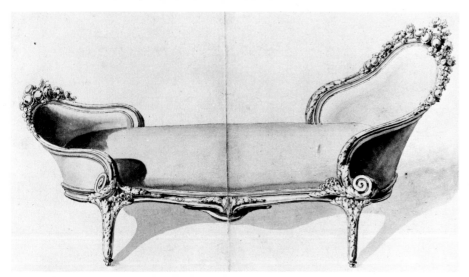

was inherited by his sons and became during the Empire period the most thriving and fashionable in Paris. The furniture produced by his second son Jacob-Desmalter is of consistently high quality, and many of his best pieces were made for the Emperor Napoleon to furnish the imperial palaces. One of the more impressive pieces of furniture made during this period was the console-table with its wide variety of supports. Superb ormolu mounts are a distinctive feature of Empire furniture, and some of the finest were produced by P. P. Thomire who had been a pupil of Gouthière.

Much of Jacob-Desmalter's furniture is closely related to the designs of the architects Percier and Fontaine whose book *Receuil de Décorations Intérieures*, published in 1801, was of such vital importance in the formation of the Empire style. In such palaces as Malmaison and the Louvre they created rooms and galleries that, while displaying grandeur sufficient to indulge Napoleon's imperial tastes, remain elegant and restrained. Another book to have considerable influence on Empire furniture was *Voyage dans la Basse et Haute-Egypte*, published by Vivant Denon (1802) on his return from Napoleon's Egyptian campaigns. This was the source of inspiration for many of the Egyptian motifs which were such a feature of the Empire style and it was also very influential in England. For more ordinary domestic furniture Pierre de La Mésangère provided some delightful designs published in *Collection de Meubles et Objets de Goût* that appeared between 1802 and 1835 in a magazine called *Journal des Dames et des Modes*.

Design for a day-bed by J. C. Delafosse. About 1775. Musée des Arts Décoratifs, Paris.

Secretaire mounted with Japanese lacquer panels attributed to Weisweiler. The mounts are possibly by Gouthière. About 1790. Rijksmuseum, Amsterdam.

One of a pair of armchairs painted in
grey, blue and pink, by Georges Jacob.
About 1785. Musée Nissim de
Camondo, Paris.

# England

## about 1760–about 1820

The Grand Tour was considered an essential part of a 'gentleman's' education during the 18th century and always included a stay of some months in Rome where he would study drawing, Classical architecture, perhaps form a collection of Antique vases or sculpture and probably have himself painted in a Roman toga by the fashionable portrait painter, Pompeo Batoni. The Grand Tour was thus instrumental in stimulating interest in the study of Classical antiquities and led in 1732 to the foundation of the Society of Dilettanti whose members were to prove such influential patrons of Neo-Classical designers and architects. Among the most distinguished of the latter was James 'Athenian' Stuart who after returning from Greece redecorated and furnished a series of rooms at Spencer House, London, between 1756 and 1765 that are regarded as being the earliest surviving Neo-Classical interiors in England.

Greece was at this time still relatively unknown, but Italy was the training ground for most of the leading architects, among them Sir William Chambers and 90 Robert Adam. Adam's aim was to create harmony in the interiors of the great houses he designed such as Kedleston Hall, Harewood House and Osterley Park House. His method of achieving this was to make every element, however small, subordinate to a ruling design. He drew his inspiration from many of the same sources as the Palladian architects, but instead of the massive scrolls, columns and entablatures used by Kent and his school, Adam introduced slender mouldings, panels of grotesques and low-relief plasterwork. He conceived of furniture as an extension of his interior architecture and not only designed each piece individually but also planned its exact position in a specific room. Thus the state rooms of a house such as Osterley Park, where most of the original furniture survives in its original positions round the walls of the room, have a strictly formal appearance, and it was not until the 19th century that furniture was pulled out into the centre of the room.

Stuart, Adam and Chambers all published architectural and furniture designs and drawings of Classical ornament that were closely studied by the principal cabinetmakers of the day, including Thomas Chippendale, Vile & Cobb, John Linnell and the firm of Ince & Mayhew. The furniture they produced in the third quarter of the 18th century began to display fluted borders, swags, paterae, tripods, vases, sphinxes and grotesques that were painted, carved or inlaid. At first such Classical ornament was merely applied to the curving forms typical of the Rococo, such as the chair 97 made by Chippendale to a design of Adam for Sir Lawrence Dundas in 1764. Soon, however, forms also began to change under the influence of Neo-Classicism, commodes became semicircular or rectangular, legs of chairs and tables straight and tapering, and the frames of pictures and looking-glasses often oval or square.

Adam's style of decoration rapidly became established in the 1770s and was carried into the following century by the architects James Wyatt and Henry Holland. Among the cabinetmakers now abandoning the Rococo in favour of 94 Neo-Classicism was George Hepple- 95 white, but as not a single piece of furni-

Lit en corbeille from La Mésangère's *Collection de Meubles et Objets de Goût,* 1807–1818.

The Dining-Room at Saltram House where Robert Adam worked on redesigning the interiors between 1768 and 1780.

ture from his workshop has been identified his fame rests entirely on his design book *The Cabinet-Maker and Upholsterer's Guide*, published in 1788 by his widow two years after his death. This book was enormously influential and includes designs for shield- and oval-back chairs, dressing-tables, secretaire-cabinets and pembroke tables that illustrate his facility for adapting the Neo-Classical style to ordinary domestic furniture.

Thomas Sheraton, like Hepplewhite, has been credited with some of the finest late 18th-century furniture, although it is doubtful whether he ever practised as a cabinetmaker. His reputation is a result of a series of design books he published between 1791 and his death in 1806: *The Cabinet-Maker and Upholsterer's Drawing Book* (1791–1794), the *Cabinet Dictionary* (1803) and the uncompleted *Cabinet-Maker, Upholsterer and General Artist's Encyclopaedia* (1804–1806). His designs are generally more original than those of Hepplewhite, but many, original to the point of bizarreness, could never have been executed. Sheraton was responsible for introducing such features as reeded supports, Egyptian figures, Grecian couches, monopodae and lion-paw feet that were to be so much employed by cabinetmakers in the Regency period, and many of his designs show French influence.

Hepplewhite is thought to have served his apprenticeship with the firm of Gillow which, with workshops in both Lancaster and London, was by this time one of the most flourishing cabinet-making concerns in England and was described by a German visitor in 1807 as producing good solid work 'though not of the first class in inventiveness and style'. Seddon & Sons was another thriving firm of cabinetmakers where at one time four hundred craftsmen were employed, including joiners, carvers, upholsterers, gilders, workers in ormolu, mirror workers and locksmiths.

Throughout the Regency period there existed a mélange of decorative styles. The Greek, Roman, Etruscan, Egyptian, Gothic, French and oriental tastes all found expression in the furniture made at this time, but in spite of this eclecticism much furniture was plainly formed. Marquetry decoration and carved orna-

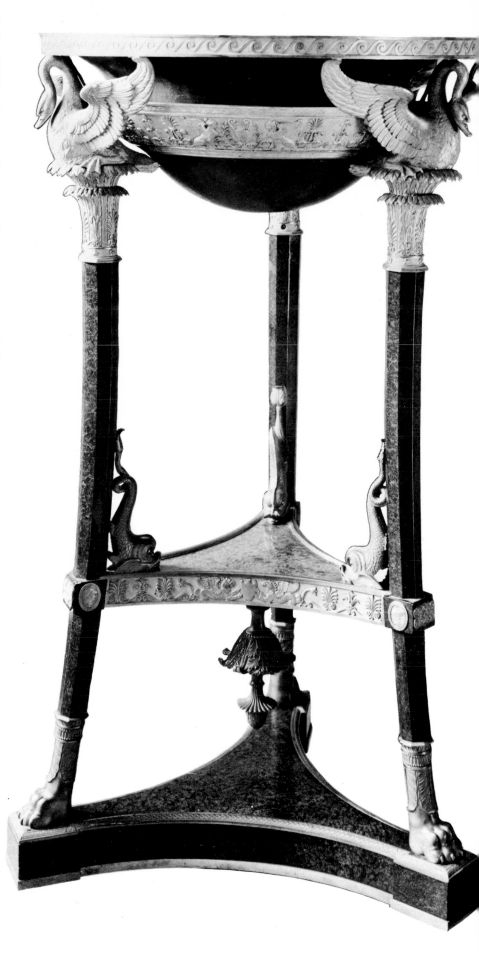

Tripod wash-stand or 'Athénienne', made after a design by C. Percier in about 1805. Château de Fontainebleau.

ment became less fashionable, and cabinetmakers relied for their effects on the striking colour and figure of such woods as amboyna, zebra-wood, maple and particularly rosewood, often combined with brass inlay.

The new generation of architects and connoisseurs studying in Italy, such as Charles Tatham who regularly sent Classical designs back to Henry Holland in England, were attempting a more accurate and archaeological approach to Antiquity. None was more single-minded in this endeavour than Thomas Hope, a wealthy collector and discerning patron whose book *Household Furniture and Interior Decoration*, published in 1807, is a

record of the decoration and furnishing of his house at Duchess Street, London. Here every element has been carefully copied from a Classical or Egyptian source and related to a central theme. Hope's furniture tends as a result to be somewhat severe, with straight lines and plain surfaces inlaid with small motifs of brass or ebony. He designed such pieces as stands in the shape of tripods, tables supported on monopodae, X-frame stools and klismos chairs. His ideas were at first too erudite for the general public but were popularised by the cabinetmaker George Smith, who in 1808 published *A Collection of Designs for Household Furniture and Interior Decoration*.

Console-table with richly carved supports showing Classical and Egyptian influences. About 1805. Louvre, Paris.

The Prince Regent, who became George IV in 1820, is one of the few English monarchs to have shown a deep interest in the arts, and although his passion for building and collecting caused the government considerable financial embarrassment, his patronage and influence were of immense importance. His summer residence, the Brighton Pavilion, has been described as the greatest monument to chinoiserie in the Western world and is certainly the ultimate expression of exoticism in the Regency period. The firm of Frederick Crace made a number of suitably oriental pieces of furniture for the Pavilion characterised by spiky outlines, applied fretwork and decoration of brightly coloured chinoiseries.

The Prince Regent employed Henry Holland, who had evolved a style of decoration that had much in common with that of Percier and Fontaine, to decorate and furnish his London residence, Carlton House (now destroyed) 95 where his taste for French art and furniture predominated. Many fine pieces of French furniture had found their way to England after the Revolution, and an expression of the French taste was the revival of boullework much encouraged by the Prince Regent and successfully produced by George Bullock. Appreciation of French art and decoration was greatly stimulated when, after the Battle of Waterloo in 1815, France was once again open to English visitors.

The Kimbolton Cabinet was made by the firm of Ince & Mayhew in 1771 to a design by Adam for the Duchess of Manchester as a frame for her set of Florentine panels of pietre dure.
Victoria and Albert Museum, London.

Sideboard similar to designs by G. Hepplewhite. About 1785.

# Germany
## about 1760–about 1830

The most outstanding German cabinet-maker of this period was David Roentgen who in 1772 took over the direction of the workshops at Neuwied which had been established by his father Abraham in 1750. David Roentgen's reputation was international, many of his most important commissions being undertaken for foreign courts, and in 1780 he was registered as a maître ébéniste by the Paris guild. His elegant Neo-Classical furniture, often built with complex mechanisms that operate secret drawers and make doors unexpectedly spring open, is remarkable for the panels of pictorial marquetry which were frequently copied from paintings by Januuarius Zick and which are among the finest creations in this medium ever produced.

Apart from Roentgen, German cabinetmakers were generally slow to embrace Neo-Classicism, and even the court cabinetmaker to Frederick the Great in Berlin was producing Rococo pieces as late as 1775. Nevertheless during the 1770s Classical ornament became increasingly apparent, and some Neo-Classical designs for furniture were published in about 1780 by Franz Heissig in Augsburg.

The impact of the French Empire style on Germany is seen in the rooms of the great German palaces, many of which were redecorated in the early 19th century. After the conflict with Napoleon had ended there was a demand for less grand and expensive furniture and for pieces that could offer comfort and practicality. Thus there developed around 1815 the Biedermeier style, distinguished for its pleasing simple lines and plain surfaces, which was to remain fashionable with the prosperous bour-

'Carlton House' writing-table. About 1800.

geoisie until the middle of the 19th century. The arrangement of rooms became gradually less formal, the deep chairs and high-back sofas, usually upholstered with horsehair and covered with velvet, being now more often pulled into the centre of the room. Work-tables, desks, china-cabinets and pianos were all familiar pieces in the comfortable drawing room of a middle class family at this period.

One of the largest and most successful cabinetmaking firms was established in Vienna under the direction of Josef Danhauser, while in Berlin the architect K. F. Schinkel designed some of the more original furniture of the period in which he combined both Classical and medieval motifs.

# Italy
## about 1760–about 1830

The finest Italian pieces made during this period continue to display the rich sculptural character that is the hallmark of so much of the best Italian furniture, and one of the most dramatic examples in this category is the table, made in 1789, now in the Vatican Library, supported on eight bronze statues of Hercules. Piranesi produced a number of designs for tables in the Neo-Classical style, and his Romantic vision of Classical ruins inspired the construction of some 'ruin rooms' in the 1750s, although sadly none appear to have survived.

Giuseppe Maggiolini, who was active in Milan during the latter part of the 18th century, was one of the few really great Italian furniture-makers who was not primarily a sculptor. Maggiolini's superb cabinets and commodes are decorated with marquetry of the highest quality using Neo-Classical designs, and they can be compared not unfavourably with the work of the ébénistes of Louis XVI.

The paucity of furniture designs produced by Italian architects and artists meant that many cabinetmakers turned to those of Hepplewhite and Sheraton for inspiration, but after the invasion of Napoleon French influence was predominant. The Empire style, with its mixture of Classical and Egyptian motifs and austere outlines, had in fact been apparent before the French invasion in 1796, but the patronage of Napoleon and his family was paramount in establishing it as the fashionable style. With French craftsmen practising in Italy and passing their skills on to Italian

Hepplewhite-style satinwood armchair. About 1785. Temple Newsam House, Leeds.

96

craftsmen, it is obviously difficult to distinguish between their respective work, a problem heightened by the fact that ormolu mounts of French origin were applied to furniture of Italian construction. Even after the fall of Napoleon the Empire style continued in vogue, but gradually from this time it became heavier and increasingly embellished with carved and gilt decoration.

An armchair from a set of chairs and sofas executed by Chippendale after a design by Robert Adam. 1764. Victoria and Albert Museum, London.

Design for a Pembroke table, plate LXII from G. Hepplewhite's *Cabinet-Maker and Upholsterer's Guide*, 1888.

# Scandinavia

## about 1760–about 1820

In Sweden and Denmark the influence of Neo-Classicism was evident as early as the 1750s. Under the direction of the French sculptor, J. F. J. Saly, the Academy in Copenhagen was the most important channel through which the Neo-Classical style was communicated to architects, artists and craftsmen. Cabinetmakers were required to present to the Academy the designs for their masterpieces, which would eventually be judged by the officers of the guild: thus high standards were constantly maintained.

The most renowned cabinetmakers of the period were the Swedish craftsmen Christopher Fürloh and Georg Haupt. After working in Paris (possibly in the workshops of Riesener) they went on to London where Fürloh remained, but Haupt returned in 1769 to Sweden where he produced some magnificent pieces in the French Neo-Classical style. The French taste continued to be dominant in Sweden, although towards the end of the century some English influences are seen, especially in the design of chair backs.

A Royal Emporium of Furniture was established in Copenhagen in 1777 with the aim of advertising the products of Danish cabinetmakers. Under the influence of Georg Roentgen (a member of the same family as David Roentgen) small oval tables became popular, and floral marquetry was much used to decorate late 18th-century pieces. In the last two decades of the 18th century, English fashions were the most influential on Danish cabinetmakers, and many fine quality mahogany pieces after the style of Hepplewhite and Sheraton have survived.

Norwegian cabinetmakers generally took a lead from the Danes, and consequently their furniture is also inspired by English examples; but in the following century this close contact between Scandinavia and England was disrupted by the Napoleonic wars. The 'Danish Empire' style is a mixture of German, English and French ideas, but despite this heavy dependence on foreign fashions, much Scandinavian furniture made during this period has a pleasing elegance and simplicity that is highly individual. The 'Late Empire' style was largely the creation of one man, the Danish designer G. F. Hetsch, who had studied under the French architect Percier, and his personal conception of Neo-Classicism influenced furniture until the middle of the 19th century. The 'Hetsch' style was also prevalent in Sweden, but about 1820 a reaction to Neo-Classicism cleared the way for the various Romantic styles and revivals that were to be current in the rest of the century.

The McIntire Bedroom of 1796–1812 at the Henry Francis du Pont Winterthur Museum, Delaware.

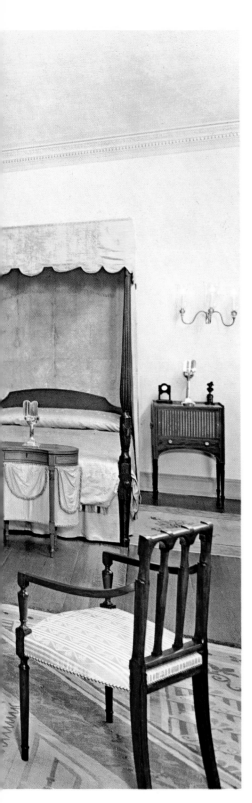

Bookcase made after a design by
T. Sheraton in the *Cabinet Dictionary* of
1803. Victoria and Albert Museum,
London.

# The Low Countries

## about 1760–about 1830

The Netherlanders' demand for French and English furniture became so overwhelming that in 1771 its importation was made illegal on the insistence of the guilds. Native cabinetmakers such as Andries Bongen were able to satisfy the public taste by producing much furniture in the French style with emphasis on marquetry decoration. They absorbed the essential elements of the Neo-Classical style, and the curves of commodes, cupboards and chairs were accordingly straightened out. Many pieces of late 18th-century Dutch furniture display lacquer panels, a feature much seen in France, but unlike the French the Dutch made little use of elaborate ormolu mounts.

In 1808 it was decided by King Louis Napoleon to convert the Amsterdam town hall into a royal palace, and in the redecoration can be seen the apogee of the Empire style in the Netherlands. After Napoleon's defeat in 1815 the Empire style continued to flourish, but in due course gave way to the Biedermeier style which persisted until the middle of the 19th century.

# Spain and Portugal

## about 1760–about 1830

In the latter part of the 18th century the influence of Hepplewhite and Sheraton designs is evident on Iberian furniture, but the strongest lead in fashion came from France and, in the case of Spain, also from Bourbon Italy. Many of the pieces produced at this period have exaggerated proportions, as in the chairs, where the seats are too large for their delicately carved backs. Chairs were often painted white or cream with gilt embellishments, but examples based on 16th-century models were also produced and sometimes decorated with japan of different colours.

There is little to distinguish Spanish furniture of the early 19th century from that of the preceding two decades, but 'Fernandino' is the name given to a style which developed after the restoration of Ferdinand VII in 1814. Fernandino designs are derived from the Empire

style; but the forms are heavier and the decoration less restrained than the French originals, and the wood employed is usually mahogany.

In view of the foreign occupation, wars and political disorders which

Sofa of 'Grecian' form. About 1820. Royal Pavilion, Brighton.

Commode made by Chippendale in about 1770 for Harewood House displaying marquetry composed of Classical motifs. Harewood House, Yorkshire.

troubled Portugal during the first quarter of the 19th century it is not surprising that no national style of furniture was evolved. But Empire and Regency styles were copied with varying degrees of skill by Lisbon furniture-makers, and after the accession in 1826 of Maria II and her German husband the influence of the Biedermeier style becomes apparent, particularly in the production of chairs.

Bed designed by F. Schinkel for Queen
Louise's bedroom in the Palace of
Charlottenburg. About 1815.
Charlottenburg Palace, Berlin.

# America

## about 1780–about 1820

Any continuing hostility felt toward the British by the young republic after the peace of 1783 did not deter Americans from importing English furniture nor their cabinetmakers from producing pieces modelled on English designs, those of Hepplewhite and Sheraton being particularly popular. The influence of Robert Adam was also very strong, and much furniture of the Federal period was inlaid or painted with Classical motifs. In this respect the eagle, being the official emblem of the new republic, achieved widespread popularity as a decorative element. New exotic woods, especially satinwood, now came into vogue.

The highboy and lowboy fell from favour, and their functions were fulfilled by chests-of-drawers and side-tables. Semicircular commodes and pembroke tables became fashionable, and the sideboard, based on Hepplewhite and Sheraton designs, made its first appearance at this time. The roll-top desk largely outmoded the fall-front type, and a break-front cabinet combined with a desk, known as a Salem secretary, was also popular. Improved communications did not stem the development of regional characteristics. Some furniture-producing towns, notably Newport, declined, while others such as Salem, New York and Baltimore, now came to the fore.

In the 1780s Salem became a flourishing port, and furniture made there was exported to places as far away as South Africa and the East Indies. Samuel McIntire is the best-known of the Salem cabinetmakers. He is particularly distinguished for his carved ornament and may have begun his career as a carver of ships' figureheads. Trailing vines, bowls, baskets and cornucopiae filled with fruit and flowers are typical motifs found on his furniture. Boston maintained its reputation for the production of fine furniture, and John Seymour and his son Thomas who were established there are famous for their beautifully veneered roll-top desks.

In New York a period of prosperity began in 1789 when George Washington started his first term as president there. Michael Allison, the firms of Stover & Taylor and Mills & Deming and the French émigré Charles Honoré Lannuier are among the foremost cabinetmakers working there, but by far the

The Red Room at the White House, furnished with pieces in the Empire style, including a round table in the background by C. H. Lannuier.

A secretaire-cabinet made in Connecticut or Rhode Island in about 1800 of cherrywood inlaid with mahogany and light woods. Henry Francis du Pont Winterthur Museum, Delaware.

most famous is Duncan Phyfe. He was enormously prolific and, as he remained in business for fifty years, a wide range of styles is reflected in his work, from English Neo-Classicism embodied in the designs of Hepplewhite and Sheraton to the French Directoire and Empire. His pieces therefore include such forms as lyre- and shield-backs, sabre legs and reeded supports and are noted for the high quality of the mahogany used in their construction. His reputation spread well beyond the confines of New York, as is shown by his commission to make a bed for Henri Christophe, King of Haiti. A coloured lithograph advertising the wares of the New York firm of Joseph
Meeks & Sons in 1833 shows furniture in the Empire style. The emphasis here is on plain surfaces, straight lines and scrolling supports, but this was only one

aspect of the Empire style in America, for much furniture in the early 19th century was heavily carved with volutes, acanthus leaves and animal paw-feet.

Cabinetmaking continued to flourish in Philadelphia. Some fine examples survive of oval and square back chairs based on Sheraton's designs with carved urn and drapery motifs. On Philadelphian cabinet furniture carving was less employed than in other centres, but large areas of contrasting veneers were used with great effect.

Baltimore now became established as an important furniture-producing town. Motifs such as bell-flowers, shells, floral and leaf designs and oval or lozenge-shaped glass panels decorated with gold and black allegorical figures painted on the reverse side are particularly associated with Baltimore pieces.

Advertisement showing furniture made by the New York firm of Joseph Meeks & Sons in 1833. Metropolitan Museum of Art, New York (gift of Mrs R. W. Hyde, 1943).

Chair made by Duncan Phyfe. About 1815. Museum of the City of New York.

# The 19th Century

## Britain
### *about 1820–about 1900*

In the aftermath of the Napoleonic wars and at a time when there was an outburst of building activity, a widespread interest developed in French furniture and decoration. After about 1825 a revival of the Louis XIV and Rococo styles [109] emerged and is well exemplified in the interiors of Belvoir Castle and Wellington's London residence, Apsley House. The Rococo gave craftsmen an opportunity to escape the more rigid disciplines imposed by the Classical styles, and elaborately carved scrolls and volutes applied to boldly curving forms of such substantial pieces as cabinets and sideboards fulfilled the early Victorian desire for opulence and ostentation.

The most dominant style of the early Victorian period was the Gothic. There was nothing startlingly new about the concept of a Gothic Revival, for there had been a continuous thread of Gothic designs for architecture and furniture since the early 18th century, and the 'Gothick' taste had been an important facet of the Regency style. However, Victorian Gothic is characterised by a new spirit of reform and a search for archaeological accuracy. The most familiar Gothic monument of this period is the Palace of Westminster (the Houses of Parliament) built between 1836 and 1860 to the designs of Sir Charles Barry and A. W. N. Pugin, the latter, by the middle of the century, being the foremost figure concerned with the Gothic Revival. The firm of J. G. Crace executed many of Pugin's designs which he published in 1835 in *Gothic Furniture*, and the severe archaeological forms and highly formalised ornament can be seen on furniture made for Abney Hall dating [108] from about 1850.

Another historical tradition to be re-

Papier-mâché tray and boxes with mother-of-pearl inlay. About 1850. Private collection.

vitalised in the 19th century was the Elizabethan style. The novels of Sir Walter Scott, such as *Kenilworth*, did much to stimulate interest in the 16th and 17th centuries, and in the decoration and furnishings of the library of Scott's house, Abbotsford, which dates from about 1820, can be seen a mixture of Tudor, Jacobean and Stuart styles. Anthony Salvin, Henry Shaw and Robert Bridgens all produced Elizabethan designs of distinction, while some fine decoration and furniture in this Romantic style survives at Charlecote Park, Warwickshire.

Victorian designers also turned to both the Italian and French Renaissance for inspiration, while Indian, Turkish and other exotic motifs can all be traced on furniture made in this period. The 'naturalistic style' describes furniture of plastic form often ornamented with sinuous carving or with panels of figurative and pictorial compositions. The woods most commonly used in the construction of early Victorian furniture are mahogany, rosewood and oak, and these were generally left plain or given the minimum of embellishment. The demand for comfort resulted in thick luxuriant upholstery that dictated rounded bulging profiles rather than straight lines. New materials gained popularity, notably papier-mâché which was no longer just reserved for small objects but now used for all kinds of furniture.

The Great Exhibition of 1851, magnificently housed in the Crystal Palace, displayed to the world the formidable progress made by British industry, but it also exposed the sadly low level of the country's creative ability in the applied arts when set in comparison with the products of Europe. The shock of this exposure was to have a stimulating and beneficial effect on British designers and craftsmen during the second half of the 19th century. Many other of the world's great cities were to follow London's example in presenting industrial trade exhibitions, and these were to exercise a powerful influence on the design of furniture: the exhibitions of Paris in 1855, London in 1862, Paris in 1867, Philadelphia in 1876 and Paris in 1900 were particularly important in this respect. Cabinetmakers of repute vied with each other to win the coveted gold medal awards, submitting special exhibition pieces, often of monumental proportions and decorated with a wealth of carving and ornament, which were designed more to impress the judges

Oak cabinet designed by A. W. N. Pugin in 1847 for Abney Hall, Cheshire. Salford City Art Gallery.

Cabinet and mirror by Jackson & Graham. 1855. Victoria and Albert Museum, London.

than to meet everyday requirements, although at the same time they showed the general trends of public taste. The firm of Jackson & Graham won a gold medal at the Paris Exhibition of 1855 for a typical exhibition piece consisting of a 108 cabinet incorporating a vast looking-glass and decorated with ormolu mounts, panels of porcelain, marble and large gilded figures. A satinwood cabinet shown at the 1867 Paris Exhibition by the firm of Wright & Mansfield is in the Adam tradition and an early example of the revival of 18th-century styles.

Furniture painted in a medieval tradition was a major innovation in the London Exhibition of 1862. The St 112 George cabinet was designed by Philip Webb and painted by William Morris in a manner inspired by examples of 13th-century Gothic chests. Philip Webb was the principal designer to the firm of Morris & Co. founded in 1861 by William Morris, who was deeply anti-pathic to the increasing use of machinery

in the production of decorative arts and who advocated a return to medieval methods of craftsmanship. One of the most splendid examples of painted furniture is an enormous bookcase de-115 signed by William Burges and painted with Christian and pagan scenes by a number of artists including Edward Burne-Jones. As well as painted decoration, gesso and panels of tooled and gilded leather were also employed to ornament furniture made by the Morris firm, while about 1860 a green stain was much used to decorate the cheaper pieces. Among the most successful products of the company were the rush-seated chairs, sold for five shillings each, that were to be widely copied by other firms.

Japanese objects had been displayed at the London Exhibition of 1862, and Japan now became a new inspiration for exotic furniture. E. W. Godwin was responsible for some of the finest designs of furniture in the 'Anglo-Japanese'

Board Room in the East Wing of the Glasgow School of Art designed by C. R. Mackintosh in 1897–1899.

Pedestal cabinet in the Rococo style. About 1850. Collection of Michael Levi 112 Esq.

style, which reached the height of its popularity about 1880

A number of William Morris's followers, A. H. Mackmurdo, W. R. Lethaby and C. R. Ashbee among them, shared his dislike for industrial art and commercial standards. They also considered the distinction between fine and decorative art to be self-conscious and invalid. With others who held similar views they set up communes of craftsmen based on the medieval guild system, where several craftsmen would work together on one piece. This became known as the Arts and Crafts Movement, and a series of exhibitions were held by their Arts and Crafts Exhibition Society between 1888 and 1899 where plain solidly made furniture was displayed with emphasis on fine and careful craftsmanship, as exemplified in the pieces designed by C. F. A. Voysey, one 110 of the most important designers concerned with this movement.

Voysey was also a major influence in the development of the Art Nouveau style that became established in the early 1890s. The whimsical flowing curves of the floral motifs associated with Art Nouveau are, however, reserved for the decoration of Voysey's furniture which is characteristically composed of strongly emphasised verticals and horizontals. The Glasgow architect Charles Rennie Mackintosh was, however, the most brilliant Art Nouveau designer in Britain, and examples of his strikingly original furniture can be seen in the Tea Rooms and in the School of Art in 109 Glasgow.

Detail of the Charlecote Park sideboard. National Trust.

*left*
Writing-desk designed by C. F. A. Voysey in 1896. The strong vertical emphasis and elaborate hinges are characteristic of his work. Victoria and Albert Museum, London.

*right*
Vitrine designed in 1898 in the manner of Emile Gallé and shown containing ornaments that were fashionable at the time. Private collection, Brighton.

# France

## about 1830–about 1900

Elements of the Neo-Classical and Empire styles persisted in French furniture long after the fall of Napoleon, but the industrial exhibition held at the Louvre in 1819 reflected a fundamental change in the furniture-making industry which was now increasingly concerned with meeting the demands of the expanding middle class for furniture which was practical and comfortable rather than with the production of works of art for noble patrons. More sophisticated machinery aided certain cabinetmaking processes such as the cutting of veneers, but increasing industrialisation combined with the lack of guild disciplines inevitably resulted in some lowering of standards. Architects no longer played such a vital part in the design of furniture, and this role was now filled by decorators, ornamentalists and upholsterers.

As in England, medieval, naturalistic and oriental styles found a ready market. The Gothic style was known in France as 'Troubadour' and was used to great effect in Princesse Marie d'Orléans's oratory in the Tuileries, while during the reign of Louis-Philippe designers also turned to the French Renaissance as a source of inspiration. A type of chair fashionable between 1830 and 1845 stood on cabriole legs and had a square or rounded back which, if not fully upholstered, was often constructed with carved cross-bars, while other examples were carved with Gothic ogee arches, trefoils and pinnacles *à la cathédrale*. A descendant of the Grecian couch that had been so popular in the Empire is the much heavier, yet no doubt more comfortable, méridienne. Light woods, particularly maple, had been fashionable in the reign of Charles X, but by 1840 dark woods such as ebony and stained oak and pear were more in vogue. Elaborate ormolu mounts were much less in evidence, and the general tendency toward smooth lines and plain surfaces seen in so much of the furniture made in the second quarter of the 19th century reflects the influence of the Biedermeier style.

One of the most distinctive features of furniture made in the reign of Napoleon III (Second Empire) is the importance of the upholstery, and an enormous variety of new upholstered seats appeared with such appealing names as indiscrets à trois places, pouffes and

The 'St George Cabinet' designed by
Philip Webb and painted by William
Morris. About 1860. Victoria and Albert
Museum, London.

Ebonised sideboard in the
'Anglo-Japanese' style designed by
E. W. Godwin in 1867. Victoria and
Albert Museum, London.

crapauds, their soft luxuriant cushions
being complemented by the heavily
draped curtains and highly patterned
wallpapers. The Gothic style continued
to be popular during the Second Empire,
its greatest protagonist being Viollet-le-
Duc, who was employed by Napoleon
III himself to restore the Château of
Pierrefonds; but there were also revivals
of virtually every recognisable style from
Francis I to Louis XVI. Boullework
became highly fashionable once more,
and other 18th-century decorative features such as inlaid porcelain plaques
and rich ormolu mounts were again
employed. During the third quarter of
the 19th century there was a vogue for
decorating different rooms in a specific

style: thus the 16th-century Henri II style is much seen in dining-rooms at this time, while the Rococo was reserved for the more feminine rooms such as the salons and boudoirs.

A reaction to all this eclecticism was given tangible expression in the foundation of the Union Centrale des Beaux-Arts which later, in 1877, became the Union Centrale des Arts Décoratifs. In an attempt to unite art and industry and to revive the status of the craftsman, its policies obviously had much in common with William Morris and the English reformers. These and other efforts to find a new source of inspiration for interior designs and furnishings came to fruition in the Universal Exhibition of 1889 where the Art Nouveau style, with its winding sinuous plant forms, melting shapes and enticing curves, was much in evidence. France produced many distinguished Art Nouveau designers, among them Emile Gallé, Eugène Grasset and the architect Hector Guimard. The dealer S. Bing was influential in disseminating the style, for he collected the whole range of articles and objets d'art needed to furnish a house in the modern manner. Such objects and furnishings were seen in a series of exhibitions during the 1890s, but Art Nouveau reached the zenith of its popularity in the Universal Exhibition held in Paris in 1900.

# Europe
## about 1830–about 1900

Throughout Europe, designers turned to past styles for inspiration, and consequently the Gothic, Renaissance, Baroque, Rococo and Neo-Classical tastes were all revived, while in Spain and Portugal the traditional national styles that had been current in the 16th and 17th centuries were also resurrected.

The Gothic Revival was popular in Germany and in Scandinavia where it appeared as early as the 1820s. In Italy, where there had never been a strong medieval Gothic tradition, designers

*top*
'Indiscret' or upholstered settee. French, about 1860. Musé des Arts Décoratifs, Paris.

*centre*
Armchair and chair characteristic of the 1840s. French. Musée des Arts Décoratifs, Paris.

Méridienne or day-bed. French, about 1830. Musée des Arts Décoratifs, Paris.

111

Painted and gilded bookcase nearly
11 feet high, designed by William
Burges between 1859 and 1862.
Victoria and Albert Museum, London.

Shaker furniture shown at the American
Museum in Britain, Bath.

preferred to work in the style of the early Renaissance which in the 19th century was known as 'Dantesque'. Typical of the pieces made in this idiom were X-frame chairs and richly carved tables. The Rococo revival was particularly fashionable in Vienna, where it first began to appear in about 1835, and is seen at its most lavish in the interiors of the Palace of Liechtenstein, redecorated in the 1840s by the firm of Carl Leistler & Son.

To some extent the quality of craftsmanship was bound to suffer as a result of increasing mechanisation and methods of mass-production; but at the same time traditional processes were often still used in the smaller workshops, and in Copenhagen and Stockholm, where there was less industrialisation than in some other European nations, a generally high standard of craftsmanship was maintained. In the 1830s in Vienna Michael Thonet was experimenting with ways of steaming and bending wood to form the structural members of chairs. Such bentwood furniture was among the earliest to be mass-produced and became popular in England after it was displayed at the Great Exhibition of 1851. The first furniture factory to be established in Holland was founded in 1853 by Matthijs and Willem Horrix in The Hague. It was immensely successful, and furniture was produced there in a wide variety of styles. A novel contribution by Dutch designers during the 19th century was the introduction of Javanese batik-work and their striking effect is seen in the furniture made by C. A. Lion Cachet in which batik designs are combined with different coloured woods.

Towards the end of the century there was a reaction to historicism largely stimulated by the pioneering reformers in England, France and Belgium. Among those seeking new forms and original materials was August Endell, one of a group of artists working in Munich who produced some examples of steel furniture, while another, Hermann Obrist, was responsible for designs reflecting the Art Nouveau style. Art Nouveau made little impact on Italy until the early 20th century, but numbers of mass-produced pieces in this style were made in the 1920s and were especially popular for the furnishing of hotels. The influence of the English Arts and Crafts Movement can be seen in the work of the Belgian artist Henry van de Velde, who settled in Germany in 1899. The spirit of reform was also strongly evident in the work of

the Viennese artists, Otto Wagner, J. M. Olbrich and Josef Hoffmann who rejected the flowing fluid lines of Art Nouveau for more functional and practical forms.

Gerhard Munthe, the Norwegian artist, produced designs for furniture that have close affinities with Art Nouveau, but he also drew inspiration from Viking decoration seen on stone carvings. Perhaps the most successful Scandinavian artist to break with historical styles was the Swedish painter Carl Larsson whose light, pleasing interiors with their bright fresh colours marked a new departure in attitudes to interior decoration that has been greatly influential in the present century.

# America
## *about 1820–about 1900*

Following European trends in fashion, American furniture was made in a variety of revival styles during this period, but at the same time new techniques led to original forms and novel methods of decoration.

The Empire style drifted on until the middle of the century, and all the designs contained in *The Cabinet Maker's Assistant* (the first American pattern book, published in 1840 by John Hall of Baltimore) reflect its influence although by now the curves and scrolls characteristic of the Empire could be far more

Centre table of rosewood in the Rococo revival style by J. H. Belter. About 1860. Museum of the City of New York.

The Library at the Gothic Revival house, Lyndhurst, New York, built in the 1840s by A. J. Davies.

easily executed with the aid of the recently invented steam-driven band-saw.

Among the most successful essays in the Gothic style, popular during the 1840s, is Lyndhurst, a house built on the banks of the Hudson river by A. J. Davis. His contemporary A. J. Downing suggested in his book *Architecture of Country Houses*, published in 1850, that the Gothic style was particularly suited to halls, bedrooms and libraries, and in America as in Europe the idea of decorating certain rooms in certain styles became widespread. The so-called Elizabethan style had a limited success between about 1830 and 1860, but furniture with twist-turned supports and applied geometric ornament is based on Jacobean and Stuart rather than Tudor examples. There were also revivals of the French Renaissance, the Baroque style of Louis XIV and the Neo-Classicism of Louis XVI, but the most fashionable of the revivals between 1850 and 1870 was the Rococo.

The most famous cabinetmaker working in the Rococo idiom was John Belter of New York. Belter's pieces are typically ornamented with intricate floral carving, and their forms achieve an extraordinary plasticity as a result of his method of construction. This consisted of laminating together up to sixteen thin layers of timber (he was especially fond of rosewood) which after steaming could be bent into the required shape. A number of other cabinetmakers made use of this process, among them Charles A. Baudoine and Alexander Roux.

In a wave of nationalism after the Philadelphia Centennial Exhibition of 1876 many reproductions of American 18th-century furniture were made, while in the 1880s and 1890s oriental and Near Eastern influences were also in evidence.

As well as these historical revivals thus briefly surveyed, new techniques and processes resulted in furniture of a very different nature. A certain amount of papier-mâché furniture was produced at Litchfield in Connecticut, while in the centres of the iron industry, Boston, New York and Baltimore, improved methods of casting led to the production of iron furniture. The search for novelty resulted in furniture made of branches or roots of trees, of cane and bamboo and, perhaps most striking of all, of animal horns. Lambert Hitchcock was one of the most successful manufacturers of mass-produced furniture and is especially remembered for his elegant 'fancy'

chairs that were assembled on a production line. Decorated with attractive stencils, they achieved enormous popularity and were sent all over America.

At the highly important Philadelphia Centennial Exhibition of 1876, chairs made by members of the Shaker religious sect won a medal for their 'Strength, Sprightliness and Modern Beauty'. It is tempting to draw parallels between the European reformers such as William Morris and the Shakers, for as far as the production of furnishings is concerned they shared many of the same ideals, and Shaker furniture is characterised by its simplicity, practicality and excellent craftsmanship.

Side chair of hickory and ash, painted black with gilt stencilled decoration, by Lambert Hitchcock. About 1830. Private collection.

# The 20th Century
## about 1900-1939

The First World War wrought profound social changes that were to revolutionise attitudes to art and design. The principal innovators working in the period just after the war were based in France, Germany and in Holland where a number of artists known as the de Stijl group (after the magazine in which they published their ideas) rejected traditional styles and turned instead to abstract geometric forms. They believed that pure simple shapes would invest their art with harmony and even a new sense of spirituality.

118 Gerrit Rietveld, a leading member of de Stijl, experimented with these principles and designed furniture of rectangular cubic construction painted only in the primary colours of red, yellow and blue, of which the 'red-blue' chair is perhaps the best-known example.

121 The ideas first formulated by de Stijl were nurtured and amplified in the Bauhaus design school founded in Germany in 1919 under the directorship of Walter Gropius. Here, too, tradition was abandoned in favour of experimentation, but at the same time students were taught to respect the requirements of function and the nature of their materials. Among the brilliant designers to emerge from the Bauhaus was Marcel Breuer who in the mid 1920s began to experiment with chrome tubing and who in 1925 produced a design for an armchair composed of light chromium plated steel tubing and canvas. Mies van
119 der Rohe, another graduate from the Bauhaus, designed the first tubular steel cantilever chair. Tubular metal was not just reserved for chairs, but was used for all kinds of furniture; and elements became standardised so that the different parts could be constructed in a variety of ways. Perhaps the most famous of Mies van der Rohe's designs is
123 that for the so-called Barcelona chair which was shown in the German Pavilion

'Red-Blue' chair designed by Gerrit Rietveld in 1917. Stedelijk Museum, Amsterdam.

at the International Barcelona Exhibition in 1929. Composed of intersecting curved bars of steel, it displays an extraordinary grace and elegance.

In France the architect Le Corbusier made a considerable contribution to furniture design. His furniture was intended to be an integral element of his interiors, and his standardised designs for chairs, tables and cabinets could be effectively placed in any of his buildings. Frank Lloyd Wright held a different

118

Armchair of chromium-plated steel tubing and canvas designed by Marcel Breuer in 1925.

view to Corbusier for, although he also felt furniture should integrate with its architectural context, he considered every house to be an individual essay, and furniture had accordingly to be designed afresh for each new building. Wright's furniture frequently reflects the architectural forms he employed, so that a polygonal room may contain polygonal furniture, while tables, benches and cabinets were often built into the structure of the house itself. His furniture designs are invariably pleasing and original, but in order to achieve his aesthetic aim he sometimes sacrificed more practical considerations.

Scandinavian artists and designers of this century have made one of the most effective contributions to the development of modern design. They did not necessarily reject the past, as is evident in the work and teaching of the Danish designer Kaare Klint, who drew inspiration from historical styles of different countries and different periods. The clean lines and sparse forms of his furniture are, however, essentially modern in conception. Klint became Professor of Furniture Design in the Architectural School of the Academy of Fine Arts in Copenhagen, and under his direction students learned to benefit from traditional styles, selecting from them their finest elements and combining them with a typically rational 20th-century approach to design. The Swedish designer Karl Bruno Mathsson produced some beautiful flowing forms with the use of laminated wood, and in Finland Alvar Aalto designed a chair in 1932 in which the seat and back are made of one piece of plywood, supported on a tubular frame.

In 1933 Aalto's furniture was displayed at an exhibition in England where the influence of continental designers was now to be seen in the production of metal furniture and pieces of cubic construction such as those designed by Wells Coates. Coates' designs and those of others such as Betty Joel and Serge Chermayeff were on view at an important show in 1933 called an 'Exhibition of British Industrial Art in Relation to the Home', that led to a more widespread knowledge of these new developments.

Scott Fitzgerald described the decade between the Great War and the Great Crash as an 'age of excess', but it also produced an individual art that has been dubbed 'Art Deco'. It is characterised by clear geometrical forms decorated

with forceful striking colours, as exemplified in the work of Pierre Legrain, who enjoyed using rare woods embellished with fine materials such as parchment, leather and lacquer. Lacquer was extremely popular in the 1920s and Jean Dumand one of the most remarkable workers in this medium.

The philosophy and teaching of the Bauhaus was totally incompatible with the Nazi regime, and in the middle 1930s many of the Bauhaus teachers and graduates, Walter Gropius, Marcel Breuer and Mies van der Rohe among them, emigrated to America where their influence was to have such a farreaching effect. Many other leading European artists and designers also chose at this time to live in America: thus on the eve of the Second World War the United States became the focal point of innovation and experiment in the realm of furniture design and interior decoration.

Interior of the Paul R. Hanna House, Palo Alto, California, designed by Frank Lloyd Wright in 1937.

Furniture designed by Walter Gropius for the Feder Store in Berlin in 1927.

Table and nest of drawers designed by
Kaare Klint in 1933.

# Glossary of Technical Terms

**acanthus.** Formalised leaf used in Classical ornament, particularly on Corinthian capitals; frequently found on furniture as carved decoration.

**anthemion.** Ornament of Greek origin based on the honeysuckle.

**arabesque.** Ornament of flowing lines composed of foliage, scrolls or animal forms, used for the decoration of borders or panels.

**arcading.** Carved decoration composed of a series of arches supported on columns or pilasters.

**architrave.** In furniture of Classical form, the lowest point of the entablature, the lintel above the columns.

**Art Nouveau.** Style of decoration which first appeared in England in the 1880s but was developed in Europe, especially in Belgium, France and Germany, in the early 1890s, then to survive some twenty years. Traditional motifs were eschewed and, instead, plant forms, waves or flame-like shapes were reflected in languid, sinuous curves expressing a new sense of abandon. The style was known in Germany as *Jugenstil*, in Austria as *Sezession* and in Italy as *Le Stile Liberty*.

**auricular ornament.** Form of decoration known in Germany as *Knorpelwerk*, in which parts of the human skeleton, surrounded by membrane and fleshy forms, were used, sometimes, as the name implies, suggesting the curving lines of the human ear. These grisly motifs appear first to have been developed by the Dutch goldsmiths, Paulus and Adam van Vianen in the first decade of the 17th century and were inspired by contemporary studies of anatomy. They were rapidly adopted as a form of decoration by carvers and cabinetmakers and did not lose popularity until the third quarter of the century.

**ball foot.** Round, ball-shaped foot forming the terminal for turned legs or the support to a cabinet or cupboard, particularly in the late 17th century.

**baluster.** Turned member of columnar form, straight, twisted, tapered or vase-shaped.

**Baroque style.** Style, based upon Classical example, which originated in Italy about 1600 and gradually spread through Europe; characterised by dynamic movement, the use of rich, symmetrical, sculptured forms and bold contrasts of colour.

**bell-flower.** American term for a conventional hanging flower bud of three or five petals used in repeated and diminishing pattern.

**bentwood.** Wood steamed and bent to form the structural members of chairs, etc.; first developed in the early 19th and widely extended in the 20th century.

**bergère** (Fr.). Large, embracing armchair with upholstered sides, popular in France in the Louis XV period and later. In England in the 18th century, these chairs were known as 'burjairs' or 'barjairs'.

**Biedermeier** (Ger.). Style of furniture and decoration current in the German territories about 1815 to 1848 in which simplicity of line and decoration was combined with a regard for function.

**block-front.** Term used to describe a technical method of constructing the fronts of case furniture, such as chests-of-drawers or cabinets, developed in America and especially in New England in the 18th century. Inspired by northern European Baroque prototypes, block fronts are composed of three flattened curves, the central of concave and the two outer of convex shape.

**blocking.** See **block-front**.

**boiserie** (Fr.). Carved wood panelling.

**bombé** (Fr.). Convex, bulging; descriptive particularly of Rococo case furniture with outward-swelling front and sides.

**bonnet scrolls.** An American term describing a curved and scrolled pediment on a bookcase, cabinet or tallboy.

**boulle** (Fr.). Term loosely used to describe a form of marquetry particularly associated with the French cabinet-maker, André-Charles Boulle (1642–1732). Veneers of tortoiseshell and brass, sometimes combined with other materials, such as pewter, copper, mother-of-pearl or stained horn, were used. Thin sheets of brass and tortoiseshell, glued together, were cut into various patterns. These were then separated, and by combining them in different ways they could be used to create two distinct marquetries. *Première-partie* describes that in which the pattern in brass is set in the ground of tortoiseshell, while *contre-partie* refers to the alternative arrangement in which the pattern is in tortoiseshell, set in the ground of brass. This system of applying marquetry was in fact not invented but developed by Boulle and was used in France throughout the 18th and the 19th centuries and copied elsewhere in Europe.

**bracket.** Member projecting from vertical surface to provide horizontal support.

**bracket foot.** Squared foot supporting the underframing of case furniture.

**breakfront.** Term used to describe a bookcase or cabinet in which the central section projects beyond the lateral sections.

**'buhl'-work.** See **boulle**.

**bulb.** The bulb-like part of the turned supports of furniture; of Flemish origin; commonly found on tables, court cupboards, etc., in the 16th and early 17th centuries.

**bun foot.** Flattened ball foot.

**cabriole leg.** Curving outwards at knee, inwards below the knee, and outwards again at the foot; terminating in feet of varied forms – hoof, club, paw, bun, claw-and-ball, scroll, etc.

**cantilever.** A projecting support or arm, carrying a load at the free end or evenly distributed along the projecting part. The cantilever principle involves the subjection to tensile stress of the upper half of the thickness of such a support, thus elongating the fibres, while the lower half is subjected to compressive stress, which tends to crush the fibres.

**capital.** The upper part of a column or pilaster, conforming in Classical architecture to the Greek (Doric, Ionic and Corinthian) and Roman (Tuscan and Composite) orders.

**carcase.** The body of a piece of furniture to which veneers are applied.

**cartouche.** Tablet in form of a scroll with curled edges, often bearing an inscription, a monogram or a coat-of-arms. Used as a decorative motif in the centre of apron pieces or pediments.

**caryatid.** Sculptured support to an entablature or moulding in form of a female figure.

**chequer ornament.** Ornamental inlay of alternating squares of light and dark woods.

**chimera.** A fabulous animal, with either a lion's or goat's body and legs, eagle's wings and a serpent's tail, used originally in Greek and Roman ornament.

**chinoiserie.** Free and fanciful rendering, in Western terms, of features adopted from the decorative repertoire of Chinese ornament. European admiration for Chinese porcelain, lacquer, textiles and wallpapers had grown rapidly in the course of the 17th century. Before the mid 18th century such motifs as latticework, frets, pagodas, bells or figures of Chinamen appeared, as an aspect of Rococo taste, in the stucco decoration of ceilings or walls and as decorative features on furniture.

**chip carving.** Shallow carved ornament usually composed of geometrical patterns, drawn with the aid of a pair of compasses and chipped out.

**Classical.** Greek or Roman and their derivatives.

**claw-and-ball foot.** Terminal to a cabriole leg in form of a paw or claw clutching a ball; of oriental derivation; widely used in England and the Netherlands in the second quarter of the 18th century and in America in the mid 18th century.

**console.** Variety of bracket, resembling a scroll, supporting the frieze or cornice of a piece of cabinet furniture. Also applied to a table standing against a wall, supported by two bracket-shaped legs.

**contre-partie** (Fr.). See **boulle.**

**cornice.** Moulded projection surmounting a frieze; the top member of an entablature.

**cusp.** Projecting point on a foiled Gothic arch, roundel, etc.

**dovetail.** A joint used in woodwork, in which fan-shaped tongues projecting from one member fit into corresponding fan-shaped slots cut in a second member.

The Barcelona chair designed by Mies van der Rohe in 1929, now manufactured by Knoll Associates Inc.

**dowel.** Wooden peg used for joining wood.

**drop-front.** See **fall-front.**

**ebonised wood.** Stained black to imitate ebony.

**Egyptian taste.** In Europe and subsequently in America the revival of Egyptian decorative motifs was stimulated by Napoleon's Egyptian campaign of 1798 and the publication of Baron Dominque-Vivant Denon's account of Egyptian antiquities, *Voyage dans la Basse et Haute Egypte.* Ornamental features which were consequently adopted included sphinxes and lotus leaves.

**entablature.** In Classical architecture, everything above the columns, i.e. architrave, frieze and cornice.

**en suite** (Fr.). As a matching set.

**fall-front.** Writing-board of a desk, lowered to form the writing surface. Also known as drop-front.

**finial.** Knob, often vase-shaped, used as a crowning ornament on furniture; also found on the intersection of stretchers joining legs of chairs, tables, etc.

**fluting.** Decoration of parallel grooves, concave and semi-circular in section, on Classical columns and friezes.

**frets.** Angular patterns, either pierced as in the galleries on tables, etc., or cut in the solid or applied, on friezes, legs, etc.

**frieze.** Horizontal section below a cornice. A cushion frieze is of convex profile.

**gesso.** A composition, often of chalk and parchment size, applied to furniture as foundation upon which gilding or silvering could be applied.

**gilding.** The decoration of surfaces with gold leaf. Woodwork was first coated with gesso before being gilded.

**Gothic style.** A style first developed in France in the mid 12th century, spreading over Europe, where it remained dominant until the Renaissance. It is characterised in architecture by pointed arches, flying buttresses, ribs, vaults and tracery in windows. The furniture of the period is also ornamented with such typical architectural features.

**griffin** (griffon, gryphon). Fabulous creature of Classical origin with an eagle's head and wings on a lion's body.

**grotesques.** Decorative design used on friezes, panels and pilasters, composed of such motifs or trailing leaves, anthemion, urns and fantastic creatures. These decorative designs were of Classical origin and were imitated and developed by Renaissance artists. As they had first been discovered on the walls of Roman ruins, or *grotti*, they came to be known as *groteschi*, hence grotesques.

**guilloche.** Carved ornament of Classical derivation consisting of interlaced circles.

**honeysuckle motif.** See **anthemion.**

**hoof foot.** Common terminal of the early cabriole leg in the form of a hoof (Fr. *pied de biche*).

**husk ornament.** Ornament resembling the husk of a wheat used in repeated and diminishing pattern, particularly on Neo-Classical furniture.

**inlay.** A surface decoration created by insetting into the solid wood a pattern or representation composed of differently coloured woods or other materials, such as ivory or horn. Inlay is recessed into a solid carcase, as opposed to marquetry, which is a veneer.

**intaglio.** Incised carving or engraving on a hard material such as a gem.

**intarsia** (or tarsia). Italian term to describe inlay or marquetry. A type of geometrical intarsia is found, for example, on Venetian 15th-century chests. At the same time, Florence was famous for intarsia panels representing pictorial scenes, while perspective views of real or imaginary architecture were popular in Italy as a whole in the late 15th and 16th centuries. At this period, too, intarsia panels for walls of furniture were skilfully produced in south German workshops.

**japanwork.** A term used in England and America to describe lacquer made in imitation of oriental lacquer. Both Chinese and oriental lacquer was widely collected by European patrons in the late 17th and earlier part of the 18th centuries, but the Japanese was of higher quality. As demand exceeded supply, European craftsmen were quick to provide for the fashion by their own efforts. English japanwork was often in bright colours such as scarlet or yellow, and much of it was exported, particularly to Portugal. Normally designs were raised on the surface, but inferior work was merely varnished.

**key pattern** (Greek fret). Repetitive pattern, of Classical origin, composed of lines set at right angles, usually applied to frieze or border.

**knee-hole desk.** Desk with central section, containing a small cupboard or drawers, recessed to allow space for the writer's knees.

**knurl foot.** Curled inwards.

**lacquer.** Essentially, decoration in coloured varnishes of oriental origin; loosely applied (with japan) to European substitutes.

**ladder-back chair.** Modern term for a chair with back composed of horizontal slats or rails.

**lambrequin.** Ornamental drapery, sometimes copied in wood, with a scalloped lower edge.

**laminated.** Composed of layers of the same or alternating materials, such as plywood or plywood faced with plastic sheets.

**linenfold.** Modern name for style of panel decoration, probably originating in Flanders in the late 15th century, and much used in the first half of the 16th century on panelled furniture, in which the carved ornament has the appearance of folded linen.

**Mannerist style.** A style evolved in Italy in the second decade of the 16th century as a reaction against the Classical tenets of the Renaissance. As a court art, adopted at Fontainebleau, it spread throughout Europe, rejecting Classical proportions and eschewing naturalistic forms.

**marquetry.** Decorative veneer of wood or other materials, such as ivory or mother-of-pearl, in which thin sheets are cut into delicate patterns and applied to the carcase. Floral marquetry, composed of trailing leaves and flowers and sometimes including birds and butterflies, was a special feature of Dutch and French cabinetmaking from the mid 17th century and was quickly copied elsewhere. In the 18th century the Parisian cabinetmakers set a new standard in the art of marquetry which was the admiration of all Europe.

**masterpiece.** Piece of work by which a craftsman gained from his guild the recognised rank of 'master'.

**mitre joint.** The corner joint of mouldings framing a panel, each edge of the join cut at an angle of 45°.

**monopodium.** Support for tables, etc., in the form of an animal's head and body with a single leg and foot; of Classical origin, revived in the late 18th and early 19th centuries.

**mortice.** Cavity into which a projecting tenon is fitted to join two pieces of wood (mortice-and-tenon joint).

**moulding.** Projecting band shaped in section, often with continuous patterning.

**Mudéjar style** (Sp.). Hispano-Mauresque style of the late 15th century evolved in Spain as a result of the influence of Moorish craftsmen who remained in the country after the fall of Granada.

**Neo-Classical style.** Style evolved in France and England in the third quarter of the 18th century and quickly adopted elsewhere in Europe and America, inspired by an increasingly informed knowledge of Roman and also of Greek art.

**ogee moulding.** Moulding of double curvature, concave below and convex above.

**ormolu.** English term, derived from the French but not, in fact, used in France, to describe decorative objects and furniture mounts of cast and gilt bronze or brass. The French term is *bronze doré*, while in England gilt bronze is an alternative description.

**oyster veneers.** Veneers cut transversely from very small branches of walnut, laburnum, olive and other trees, showing the whorled pattern of the graining, and laid side by side, a method developed in Holland in the second half of the 17th century.

**pad foot.** Resembling club-foot, but set on a disc.

**'paintbrush' foot.** American term to describe the foot of a chair or table curled inwards in resemblance of a paintbrush; otherwise known as tassel foot, or Spanish foot *(pie de pincel)*.

**palmette.** Ornament of formalised palm leaf, of Classical derivation, often resembling a spread fan.

**papier-mâché.** Process of ancient Eastern origin, later developed in France and elsewhere, by which specially prepared paper pulp, mixed with other ingredients, is pressed, moulded and baked into a hard substance used in furniture and capable of taking a high polish.

**parcel gilt.** Partly gilt.

**parquetry.** A form of veneer, creating a geometrical pattern.

**passementerie.** Lace-work or trimming.

**patera.** A motif of Classical origin, consisting of a round or oval decoration; much used in the Neo-Classical period, applied, carved, inlaid or painted.

**pedestal.** In architecture a moulded base supporting a column. In terms of furniture, a solid support for a lamp or a decorative object. Pedestal desks are those in which the top is supported on two side sections containing drawers. Pedestal tables are supported on a single pillar or column.

**pediment.** Member of triangular or curved form surmounting a Classical cornice. When 'broken', the lines of the pediment are stopped before reaching the apex.

**pietre dure** (It.). Ornamental work in hard stone (e.g. jasper, agate), originating in Florence in the late 16th century. Widely used for table tops and decorative cabinets from that period.

**pilaster.** Flattened column, rectangular in section.

**Plateresque.** Descriptive of exuberant early Renaissance decoration on Spanish furniture; name first applied to such decoration on silver *(plata)*.

**press.** A cupboard.

**putto** (It.). Naked male infant much used as a decorative motif on furniture from the Renaissance.

**reeding.** Convex moulding resembling series of reeds; the exact opposite of fluting.

**Régence period** (Fr.). Term most commonly used to describe the years between 1715 and 1723 when Philippe, Duc d'Orléans, was Regent of France during the minority of Louis XV.

**Rococo** (Rocaille). Derived from the French *rocaille*, the term describes a style which originated in France in the early 18th century and spread throughout Europe. A decorative style conceived at first in terms of flowing arabesques, it developed in the second quarter and in the mid 18th century a more sculptural volatile manner, in which motifs based on shell and rock forms, foliage, flowers, sprightly animals, 'C'-scrolls and tortuous curves were combined with fantasy and charm.

**roll-top desk.** A desk closed by means of a flexible shutter of convex shape composed of strips of wood. See also **tambour front.**

**Romanesque.** Style currently in Europe in the 11th and 12th centuries characterised by the round arch inspired by Classical example.

**roundel.** Ornament occupying a circular space.

**sabre leg.** A leg curved in resemblance of a cavalry sabre.

**Scagliola** (It.). Composition of plaster and glue, to which small pieces of marble were added, coloured to imitate marble and other ornamental stone; capable of taking a very high polish.

**sconce.** Wall light.

**serpentine form.** A profile composed of a convex curve, flanked by two concave curves.

**sphinx.** Hybrid monster with the head of a woman and the body of a lion.

**splat.** Vertical member between the uprights of a chair back; often pierced or shaped.

**split baluster** or spindle. Turned member split lengthwise and applied as matched decoration on furniture.

**spoon-back.** American term to describe a 'Queen Anne' chair with a back curved like a spoon to give comfort to the sitter.

**strapwork.** Decoration composed of interlacing bands or straps sometimes combined with foliage. A popular ornament in northern Europe in the second half of the 16th and early 17th centuries. Late 17th-century Baroque ornament also included a delicate form of foliate strapwork based upon the designs of the French designer, Jean Berain.

**stretcher.** Horizontal bar joining and strengthening the legs of chairs or tables.

**stucco** (It.). Plaster.

**tambour front.** A roll front or shutter made of narrow strips of·wood glued to a canvas backing, and used for desk tops, etc.

**tester.** Wooden canopy, particularly over a bedstead.

**'thrown' chair.** 16th-century chair with triangular seat and arms, the legs and back composed of turned members.

**trefoil.** An ornament suggesting a three-lobed leaf.

**trompe l'oeil** (Fr.). A pictorial technique, using perspective and foreshortening, to deceive the eye and heighten the impression of reality.

**Troubadour style.** (Ironic) description in France in the 19th century of furniture in the revived Gothic style.

**turkeywork.** Upholstery of even, deep pile formed by knotting wools on a canvas base, in imitation of Turkey carpets. In use from the 16th century onwards.

**turning.** Until about 1700 turning was an outstanding feature of chair and table legs. It was executed on a foot-operated pole lathe, and the turner's chisel determined the final shape. Baluster turning resulted in turned members of various columnar shapes (see **baluster**). Ball-and-spool turning and bobbin-turning were other popular 17th-century characteristics, the members imitating the shapes of spools or bobbins. Twist- or spiral-turning, resembling 'barley sugar', was sometimes known by this latter name.

**veneer.** Thin sheet of wood glued to the carcase of furniture for decorative effect; formerly sawn by hand, now cut by machine.

**vernis martin** (Fr.). Term used generically to describe varnishes and lacquers used for furniture and interiors in France in the 18th century. The four Martin brothers developed a method of lacquering (patent 1730, renewed 1744) which brought them court patronage and widespread fame. They used many colours, but their green lacquer was the most celebrated.

**vitrine** (Fr.). Display or china cabinet.

**Vitruvian scroll** (wave pattern). Border decoration of Classical origin composed of a band of convoluted scrolls.

**volute.** Spiral scroll, particularly associated with Ionic capital.

**wainscot.** Name originally used in medieval England for imported timber suitable for wagon (wain) construction, and thus for furniture and panelling; more strictly applied in America to panelling and panelled furniture.

124